US NAVAL AVIATION

F11F-1 Tigers of the 'Blue Angels' flight demonstration team passing over San Francisco's Golden Gate bridge. The Navy's first carrier-based supersonic fighter, the Tiger equipped the 'Blues' for a period longer than any other aircraft, from April 1957 to 1969.

Grumman

US NAVAL AVIATION

1946–1999

MARTIN W. BOWMAN

SUTTON PUBLISHING

First published in 1999 by
Sutton Publishing Limited · Phoenix Mill
Thrupp · Stroud · Gloucestershire · GL5 2BU

British Library Cataloguing in Publication Data
A catalogue record for this book is available from the British Library

ISBN 0 7509 2175 7

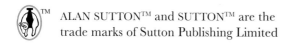
Typeset in 11/15 pt Baskerville.
Typesetting and origination by
Sutton Publishing Limited.
Printed in Great Britain by
Butler and Tanner, Frome, Somerset.

INTRODUCTION

US Maritime power, not just for the protection of the United States but for projection of American power around the world, has its beginnings in the Pacific, 1941–5. Starting with the decisive battles of Coral Sea, 7–9 May 1942, and Midway, carrier-borne aircraft progressively rolled back the Japanese onslaught in the Pacific. In the western hemisphere, too, the US Navy was decisive against Axis forces in Atlantic waters and the Mediterranean Sea. Overwhelming victories against the Imperial Japanese Navy at Guadalcanal, the Marianas, and Okinawa all but erased the black memory of Pearl Harbor. By 1945 America possessed a navy more powerful than any other in history – one which had almost completely annihilated her maritime opponents.

Post-war, America benefited greatly from German wartime aero-nautical research, and equally importantly, the British lead in jet engine and carrier technology. On 21 July 1946 the McDonnell FD-21 prototype Phantom had become the first US pure-jet landing aboard an aircraft carrier when it landed on USS *Franklin D. Roosevelt*. In March 1948 the FJ-1 Fury had become the first USN jet fighter to go to sea under operational conditions. Britain no longer ruled the waves but every innovation aboard carriers, from the angled flight deck to the mirror landing sight, has British ancestry.

As the Cold War fight against communism intensified, America could not afford to lag behind, especially when the first military confrontation between east and west, in Korea, became a battleground on 25 June 1950. An uneasy peace in the Land of the Morning Calm was shattered when the North Korean Army crossed the 38th Parallel, completely wrong-footing the South and its American advisors. America was largely unprepared in conventional military terms and the North enjoyed total air superiority from the outset. US commanders had had no reason to fear the Communist air threat because only piston-engined aircraft confronted them. The Grumman F9F-2 Panther was the Navy's first-line carrier-borne jet fighter throughout the first year of the war and was powered by the same 5,000 lb thrust Rolls-Royce Nene engine! On 3 July 1950 Panthers had been the first jet fighters in the USN to go into action when thirty from VF-51 provided top cover for the carrier's Skyraiders and F4U Corsairs that bombed targets near the North Korean capital, Pyongyang. When China entered the war on the North Korean side and, on 1 November 1950, American aircraft were confronted by the MiG-15 for the first time, the balance of air power in Korea was decisively altered at a stroke. The MiG-15 was the result of a Soviet project in 1946 that benefited from German research into swept wings and the Nene turbojet, of which twenty-five were sold to the Soviets under the Anglo-Soviet Trade Agreement of 1946. Early production MiG-15s were powered by an RD-45F centrifugal-flow turbojet copied from the Rolls-Royce engine.

USAF aircraft were ill-suited to operate in a close air support and interdiction campaign in Korea. They needed paved runways 6,000 ft long and these only existed in Japan, which meant that air operations over Korea were restricted to only a few minutes. The US carriers, therefore, were essential during the long, gruelling campaign, which was to last thirty-eight months. Navy units could operate in the Sea of Japan and be sent off from about 70 miles from the coast of Korea (the shallow sea bed off the east coast of Korea prevented them from getting any nearer). On 27 July 1953 the Communists finally signed an armistice and peace reigned once again in the Land of the Morning Calm.

In 1954 the Navy went supersonic when the F11F-1 Tiger became the first super-sonic operational carrier-borne naval interceptor in the world. The Navy replaced its F9F Panther and F2H Banshee straight-winged jets with the F-4 Phantom, and the Vought F-8 Crusader became the standard carrier-based fighter but propeller-driven aircraft, like the Douglas A-1 Skyraider, still had a role to play. In February 1958 USS *Enterprise*, the world's second nuclear-powered surface warship, powered by eight reactors, was laid down. She was commissioned in November 1961. Ed Heinmann's Douglas A-4 Skyhawk was designed to replace the Skyraider and fulfil a multiplicity of roles for the Navy, including interceptor and nuclear weapons carrier, but for a while both aircraft served alongside each other as hostilities, which had been simmering in South-east Asia for years, escalated into full-scale war in Vietnam in the early sixties.

In 1961 'special advisors' were sent to South Vietnam and President Lyndon B. Johnson began the first moves that would lead to total American involvement in Vietnam. In 1964 two F-8 Crusaders were downed over Laos. On 2 August the Seventh Fleet was involved in an incident with North Vietnamese torpedo boats in the Gulf of Tonkin. In February 1965 the first American casualties occurred when the Viet Cong attacked US installations in the South. In retaliation, FLAMING DART I, a strike from carriers in the Gulf of Tonkin, took place. In March Operation ROLLING THUNDER, an air offensive against North Vietnam, was launched, the Navy's first strike taking place on 18 March. In April 1965 the pattern for the rest of the conflict in South-east Asia was established when Chinese MiG-17 jets were introduced.

Early in 1968 President Johnson forbade all strikes further than the 19th Parallel and on 1 November he ordered a halt to all bombing of North Vietnam. The bombing was only resumed in May 1972, when the North Vietnamese offensive prompted President Nixon to authorize the LINEBACKER I all-out offensive against the North. Navy operations reached a peak in May when nearly 7,250 sorties were flown at a time when six carriers – the most on line in the conflict – were operating in the Gulf of Tonkin. During LINEBACKER I, which ended in October 1972, just over 23,650 sorties were flown against North Vietnam. LINEBACKER II, to which the Navy again contributed six air wings, ran from 18 to 26 December 1972, and finally forced the Communists to declare a cease-fire on 23 January 1973. Inevitably, the South soon collapsed, and on 12 April 1975 the American Embassy in Saigon was evacuated and 287 staff were flown to carriers offshore. On 29 April a further 900 Americans were airlifted by the Navy to five carriers. Next day Saigon was in Communist hands and the South was now under the control of North Vietnam. In May 1975 the USN airlifted US nationals and personnel from Saigon in Operation FREQUENT WIND.

By the mid-1980s the USN had in service twelve carrier air wings aboard the same number of carriers. Each air wing could muster eighty or more aircraft. The Sixth Fleet, in the Mediterranean, proved a very efficient avenger, and then deterrent, in the fight against international terrorism with raids against Libyan and Lebanese targets. In February 1986 Operation PRAIRIE FIRE was launched to provoke Libya into a direct military confrontation. On 14 April 1986 Operation EL DORADO CANYON, the bombing of terrorist-related targets at Tripoli and Benghazi, went ahead. USAF F-111Es based in Britain, and carrier-borne aircraft in the eastern Mediterranean, hit Libyan targets in Tripoli and in and around Benghazi. Operation PRAYING MANTIS against Iranian naval vessels in the Arabian Gulf went ahead on 18/19 April 1988.

On 2 August 1990 President Saddam Hussein of Iraq massed seven divisions and 2,000 tanks along the Iraq–Kuwait border and they invaded Kuwait in the early morning hours. DESERT SHIELD began with warplanes and ground forces sent to Saudi Arabia, while America's huge carrier battle groups were placed on full war alert, each carrier carrying up to nine squadrons – fighter, medium attack, light attack, anti-submarine warfare (ASW), electronic warfare (EW) and Airborne Early Warning (AEW). On 16 January 1991 Operation DESERT STORM began with all-out attacks by land-based strike aircraft and by naval units at sea. The war began during the night of 17 January, with the launching of fifty-two Tomahawk land-attack cruise missiles from the battleship *Wisconsin* and other surface ships. President George Bush announced a cease-fire on 28 February 1991. The USN averaged 125 to 150 sorties per day per carrier (weather permitting). Operations were flown by day and by night with about half the sorties being strike missions.

By 1992 fourteen carriers were in service. In 1990 commissioning of fifth and sixth *Nimitz* class nuclear-powered multi-role carriers took place. The ten *Nimitz* class carriers built are powered by two nuclear reactors and can run for more than a decade 'on the same tank of gas'. The *Nimitz* class carriers are scheduled to serve until at least 2020. Like the rest of the fleet, they remain ever vigilant, ready to strike when diplomacy fails.

ACKNOWLEDGEMENTS

I would like to thank: Lieutenant Commander David J. Albritton USN; the late Roland H. Baker; Lieutenant Commander Brent D. Chénard USN, and all the Public Affairs officers aboard USS *John F. Kennedy*; Lee Cook; Robert Cressman; Dept of the Navy-Pentagon; Graham Dinsdale; Captain Edward J. Fahy Jr., and crew of the *John F. Kennedy*; Thomas J. Fitton; Bob Gaines; Philip Jarrett; Lieutenant Christopher J. Madden USN; McDonnell Douglas; Hunter Reinburg; Jerry C. Scutts; Roger Seybel, Grumman History Center; Graham M. Simons; Brynell Somerville; Captain Armistead 'Chick' Smith USN (Retd); Peter C. Smith; Captain Paul F. Stevens USN (Retd); Terry Treadwell; Walt Truax; Henrietta Wright, Dept of the Navy-Pentagon. Thanks also to the dedicated staff of the US 2nd Air Division Memorial Library in Norwich.

Two huge 92 ton, double-decker Lockheed XR60-1 (XR6V-1) Constitutions, each capable of carrying 180 persons, were constructed as Navy transporters in 1946. The first of two XR60-1s (BuNo85163) flew on 9 November 1946. Both aircraft were delivered in 1949 but they were found to be under-powered and to have insufficient range and the type never entered production.

Lockheed

Design work on the Lockheed P2V (P-2) Neptune was begun in September 1941 but war intervened and the first XP2V-1 (26–1001) was not completed until the spring of 1945. It flew for the first time on 17 May 1945 but the end of the war caused orders for 100 of the aircraft to be cancelled. However, on 13 September 1946, Lockheed received an order for thirty P2V-2s and the onset of the Cold War, and the Korean War, saw an upsurge in orders that kept the aircraft in production until spring 1962. BuNo89082 *The Turtle* (pictured), the first P2V-1, was modified during construction in an attempt to set a new world distance record. During the period 26 September to 1 October 1946 *The Turtle* established a world non-stop, unrefuelled flight record when Commander (later Rear Admiral) Thomas D. Davies, his three crew (and a kangaroo!) covered the 11,236 miles from Perth, Australia, to Columbus, Ohio, in 55 hours 17 minutes! It had taken off with 8,396 gallons of fuel and 85,500 lb of gross weight. This record stood for sixteen years until it was broken by a B-52H.

Lockheed

A Douglas A2D-1 Skyshark, which flew on 26 May 1950. Two prototypes and ten production Skysharks were built but protracted powerplant and related gearbox problems and the emergence of the XA-4D-1 Skyhawk saw all further Skyshark development cancelled.

Douglas

First conceived late in the Second World War as a successor to the Avenger, the Grumman Design 70 (XTB3F-1/BuNo90504) Guardian flew on 23 December 1946. Next day, Christmas Eve 1946, the USN ordered work on the XTB3F programme to stop. (The more adaptable Douglas AD-1 and Martin AM-1 were planned to operate both in the bombing and torpedo bombing roles so the Navy no longer needed a large multi-seat torpedo bomber.) However, the USN sought a replacement for the TBM-3W/TBM-3S hunter-killer team in the carrier-borne ASW role so Grumman was instructed to complete XTB3F-1 BuNo90505 as the XTB3F-2S ASW prototype, and the third prototype (BuNo90506) as the XTB3F-1S ASW search aircraft prototype with AN/APS-20A radar. The three-seat AF2S killer (top) was adopted in March 1948 and the four-seat AF-2W hunter designation (foreground) in July 1979.

Grumman

AF-2S BuNo123090 with full external load consisting of an AN/APS-31 radar and an AN/AVQ-2 searchlight in underwing nacelles, two 150 gallon drop tanks, and six High Velocity Aerial Rockets (HVARs). The AF-2W *Guppy* and AF-2S *Scrapper* worked as hunter-killer, the AF-2W flying at low altitudes, searching the surface for a submarine periscope or snorkel. When the AF-2W had located the target, an accompanying AF-2S pinpointed it with an APS-31 radar under the starboard wing. If it surfaced at night, the submarine could be illuminated with the searchlight under the port wing; if submerged, the target was located with sixteen sonobuoys. The AF-2S could make its attack with a 1,167 lb Mk 34 torpedo carried in the weapons bay, or with four depth-charges carried under the wings. Up to six rockets could be carried under the wings in place of the depth-charges or drop tanks.

Grumman

The first AF-2S and AF-2W Guardians were issued to VX-1 development squadron at NAS Key West, Florida, in June 1950 and Board of Inspection and Survey (BIS) carrier trials took place aboard USS *Wright* (CVL-49, pictured in November 1950). Initial carrier operations were made on board USS *Palau* (CVE-122) by VS-24 in December that year. Guardians first entered service with VS-25 at San Diego, California, in October 1950. By April 1953 as many as 193 AF-2S, 153 AF-2W and 40 AF-3S Guardians had been delivered, the latter with AN/ASQ-8 magnetic anomaly detector (MAD). Guardians went on to equip eleven fleet squadrons from late 1950, providing effective ASW support to Task Force 77 (TF-77) during the Korean War. The last Guardians were retired from squadron service in August 1955, when they were replaced by Grumman S-2 Trackers .

Grumman

America first captured the world's absolute speed record on 19 June 1947 when the Lockheed XP-80R Shooting Star, piloted by Colonel Albert Boyd, USAAF, reached 623.74 mph at Muroc (later Edwards AFB), California. Meanwhile, a joint USN/NACA project resulted in Navy Project Officer Commander Turner F. Caldwell (pictured) eclipsing this record on 20 August 1947 when he achieved an average speed of 640–63 mph in the first D-558-1 Skystreak, BuNo37970. Caldwell's record lasted just five days; Major Marion Carl, USMC, broke the record in the second Skystreak with a speed averaging 650–796 mph.

Douglas

Commander Turner F. Caldwell with famed Douglas aircraft designer Ed Heinemann study a model of the D-558-1 Skystreak.

Douglas

In 1948 three new D-558 models, called 'Phase Two' aircraft, with swept wings, were built. Particular attention was given to the problem of 'pitch up', a phenomena often encountered with swept-wing configured aircraft. Four P2B-1S (B-29-BW) aircraft were obtained by the USN in 1947 (one pictured, on 4 February 1948). In November 1953 Scott Crossfield became the first man to fly faster than twice the speed of sound after his D-558-II had been released from a P2B-1S.

Douglas

F8F-1 BuNo95337 flown by Pat Gallo from Bethpage, New York, 1945. On 31 December 1944 the first production F8F-1 powered by a R-2800-34W single-stage, two-speed supercharged radial was delivered to the Navy. Designed to replace the F6F and operate from even the smallest of carriers against *Kamikaze* attacks in the Pacific, the F8F only began replacing the Hellcat in fleet service during May 1945, when F8F-1s of VF-19 were embarked aboard the light carrier *Langley*. Originally, a contract was placed with Grumman on 6 October 1944 for 2,023 F8F-1s but the war ended before combat deployment in the Pacific, by which time only 151 examples had been built.

Grumman

F8F-1 BuNo95318 flown by Lieutenant Commander
D.E. 'Whiff' Caldwell, CO of VF-20, which was one of
eight squadrons to receive Bearcats in 1946, photographed
over San Francisco, California, on 2 June 1947 by William
T. Larkins. By 1947 nineteen squadrons were equipped
with Bearcats, and by 1948 twenty-four squadrons were
operating F8Fs. F8F-1 production finished on 29 August
1949 with only 765 F8F-1s being built, while an order
placed with Eastern Aircraft Division of General Motors
on 5 February 1945 for 1,876 F3M-1 Bearcats was
cancelled before production began.

William T. Larkins

Opposite and above: An F8F-1 groundloops into two other Bearcats aboard USS *Tarawa*. (Wrecked aircraft at sea were usually 'deep-sixed' – pushed over the side to six fathoms.) Bearcats equipped thirty-two Navy squadrons at one time or another during 1945 to 1949. In 1946 an order for 126 cannon-armed F8F-1B carrier-based fighter-bombers was issued and modifications to thirty-six F8F-1s and F8F-1Bs (to include APS-19 radar suspended from a pylon on the starboard wing) resulted in the F8F-1N night-fighter. The Bearcat did not serve in the Korean conflict because it lacked the F4U Corsair's weapons load-carrying capability and the jet's performance, despite a top speed of 447 mph at 28,000 ft.

Grumman

Grumman received a contract on 28 June 1946 for 365 F8F-2s (BuNo121612 is pictured), twelve of which were night-fighter versions. The F8F-2 flew on 11 June 1947, powered by a Pratt & Whitney 2,250 hp R-2800-30W variable-speed supercharged engine equipped with water injection and an automatic engine control unit. The aircraft also had a 12 inch extension to the vertical fin to improve stability. A 150 gallon droppable fuel tank could be installed on the fuselage bomb rack and a 100 gallon droppable tank on each wing bomb rack.

Grumman

From 26 February 1948 to 31 May 1949, sixty F8F-2s were modified to F8F-2P photo-reconnaissance versions (BuNo121580, the first, is pictured), fitted with two 20 mm wing guns instead of four. It was not until late 1952 that the last F8F-2P squadron gave up its Bearcats.

Grumman

In December 1945 the USN invited proposals for a turboprop flying boat using the new hull shapes under development, and Convair responded on 19 June 1946 with two XP5Y-1 prototypes powered by four complex 5,100 shp Allison XT40-A-4 propeller-turbines driving six-blade contra-rotating propellers (each T40 consisting of two T38s coupled together). Finally, after a long delay caused by powerplant problems, the P5Y-1 made its first flight, from San Diego Bay, on 18 April 1950. Originally, the specification called for defensive armour to be fitted but, by now, the primary mission was changed to ASW and, later still, to mine-laying, and the five pairs of 20 mm guns that were to be mounted on remotely controlled turrets were abandoned. The engine problems were never solved, the second prototype crashed on 15 July 1953, and the only eleven R3Y-1 Tradewind transport versions were built. These were retired in January 1958 following the loss of one of the R3Ys. The Tradewind was Convair's last flying boat, last patrol type, and the only USN turboprop boat.

Convair

The Grumman SA-16 (G-64) Albatross was initially intended as a utility amphibian with a crew of five or six and accommodation for twenty-two passengers. Ordered in 1944, the XJR2F-1 (Pelican) prototype first flew on 1 October 1947, and the Albatross entered military service in July 1949. A total of 466 of these versatile amphibians were built from September 1947 to May 1961, and were delivered to the US Air Force, Navy, and Coast Guard, as well as many overseas air forces. UF-1 (HU-16C) BuNo141289 (pictured) was one of ninety-four UF-1s built.

Grumman

Ordered on 22 March 1945, the McDonnell F2H-1 Banshee single-seat fighter was similar in design and appearance to the FH-1 Phantom, but was powered by the larger and more powerful 3,250 lb thrust Westinghouse J34 turbojet. The XF2H-1 (BuNo99859, the second of three XF2H-1 prototypes, is pictured) first flew on 11 January 1947. Some fifty-six production F2H-1s ordered on 29 May 1947 were delivered from August 1948 to July 1949. F2H-1s began service operation with VF-171 in March 1949.

McDonnell

The F2H-2 Banshee that appeared in 1949 had more powerful engines, increased internal fuel and a 200 gallon drop tank on each wing tip (pictured is XF2H-1 BuNo99859 with 200 gallon drop tanks fitted).

McDonnell

Gleaming F2H-2 Banshees coming off the McDonnell production lines. Altogether, 895 'Old Banjos' were built from winter 1949 to 1953. Some 364 F2H-2s were delivered during the period November 1949 to September 1952, plus fourteen F2H-2Ns with APS-6 radar installed in the nose as carrier-based night-fighters, and eighty-nine F2H-2P photo-reconnaissance models were also built. Twenty-five F2H-2s were modified during construction with strengthened wings and hardpoints for bombs to F2H-2B standard in order to carry a Mk 7 or Mk 8 nuclear bomb under the port wing.

McDonnell

An F9F-3 Panther of VF-51 'Screaming Eagles' lands on USS *Boxer* (CV-21) in September 1949, during the first West Coast carrier operations. VF-51 was the first to receive the Panther-jet when it replaced its FJ-1 Furys in May 1949, and was the first to operate jets from a carrier when it began operations from *Boxer* in September. A Rolls-Royce 5,000 lb thrust Nene was installed in the first XF9F-2, which flew on 24 November 1947. The XF9F-3 flew on 16 August 1948, powered by a 4,600 lb thrust Allison J33-A-8, similar in size to the Nene. Contracts for forty-seven F9F-2s with the Pratt & Whitney J42-P-6 version of the Nene, and fifty-four F0F-3s with Allison J33-A-8s, followed. Since the powerplants were not interchangeable, after October 1949 all the F9F-3s were converted to F9F-2s.

Grumman

An F9F-2 Panther of VF-51 'Screaming Eagles' lands on USS *Boxer*, October 1949. When the Korean War erupted VF-51 was aboard *Valley Forge*, or the 'Happy Valley' as it was known, in the Pacific.

Grumman

After a mini-blockade lasting from April to June 1948, the Soviets cut off road, rail and barge traffic between Berlin and the Western occupation zones of Germany on 24 June. The Berlin Airlift began two days later when the USAF started flights from Frankfurt and two other bases using C-47s and C-54 Skymasters. Two USN squadrons, VR-6 and VR-8, were deployed on 27 October. The first R5D (USN version of the C-54D) arrived at Rhein-Main on 9 November, flying its first airlift mission four hours later. At the peak of operations, 204 C-54s and 22 R5Ds were in operation into and out of Berlin (Tempelhof) in the US zone, and Gatow in the British zone. Here, air and ground crews of VR-6 at Rhein-Main celebrate the end of the blockade, 12 May 1949. The airlift continued until the end of September 1949.

USN

TBM-3W BuNo69476 from NAS Boca Chica, near the Florida Keys, 30 January 1950. The -3W was a result of Project 'Cadillac', an over-the-horizon AEW system first developed at the end of the Second World War. All armament and armour was removed and the Avenger was fitted with a large ventral radome to house the APS-20 radar. By June 1948 the first AEW squadron, VC-2, was activated with TBM-3Ws. Externally similar to the -3W but with improved radar capable of detecting the snorkel of submerged submarines, TBM-3W2s entered service in the summer of 1950.

Grumman

TBM-3Ws of Naval Reserve Squadron VS-833 at NAS New York at Floyd Bennett Field in 1954. The last four TBM-3Ws were phased out of front-line service in the summer of 1951, and TBM-3W2s were the last Avengers in US military service, finally being withdrawn from the Reserve at the end of 1956.

Grumman

TBM-3E2 BuNo91281 of Reserve Squadron VS-833, NAS New York, being flown by Lieutenant R. Hassler, photographed by Roger Seybel on 17 October 1954. The -3E was the last Avenger model to enter production during the Second World War. It had a fuselage lengthened by 11½ inches and carried an AN/APS-4 search radar in a radome beneath the starboard wing. The 3E2 designation was applied to aircraft that were modernized after the war, the majority of which had the original 'stinger' arrester hook replaced by an external hook located beneath the tail.

Grumman

At the start of the Korean War, 25 June 1950, when Communist North Korea poured across the 38th Parallel, *Valley Forge* (CV-45) and CVG-5 (Air Group Five), the most experienced jet air group in the Navy, comprised the only carrier force in the Western Pacific. (Only fifteen carriers were now in commission.) For her first tour of duty off the south and eastern coasts of Korea, 5 August 1950 to February 1951, *Philippine Sea* (CV-47, pictured) joined CV-45 in providing close air support (CAS) and interdiction of enemy supply lines as North Korean forces attempted to break through the Pusan perimeter.

Roland H. Baker

Before sailing from San Diego, California, on 5 July, CV-47 had embarked CVG-11; two F9F-28 squadrons, VF-111 and VF-112; two F4U-4 fighter-bomber squadrons, VF-113 and VF-114; an AD-4 Skyraider squadron, VA-115; plus detachments from CV-3, VC-11, VC-35 and VC-61. CVG-11 had not yet finished its training cycle, as its two jet squadrons had just received its F9F Panthers. Arriving at Oahu, Hawaii, on 10 July 1950, CV-47 conducted intensive Carrier Qualifications (CarQuals).

Roland H. Baker

Opposite, above: Ordnancemen on board *Philippine Sea* load 250 lb bombs onto the wings of an AD-4 Skyraider. Conceived during the Second World War as the XBT2D-1, the Skyraider became the AAD-1 on 11 March 1946 when the Navy replaced the VB (dive) and VT (torpedo) designations for its bombers with 'VA' for 'attack' aircraft. Deliveries began in November 1946 of the first of 242 'Able Dogs', as the AD-1 was called, and thirty-five AD-1Q radar-countermeasures versions. All 372 AD-4s built were fitted with four 20 mm guns with 200 rounds, but faulty guns caused by the extremely low temperatures at altitude were a common and frustrating problem. AD-4s could carry 2,000 lb bombs, torpedoes, or drop tanks on the main pylons, while outer-wing stations were used for 500 lb bombs or rockets, with a maximum capacity of up to 6,500 lb operating from a carrier. During the Korean War twenty-four Navy Skyraider squadrons were operational.

Roland H. Baker

Below: In *Philippine Sea*'s Wardroom on 5 August 1950, Rear Admiral Edward C. Ewen and Commander W. 'Sully' Vogel Jr. (aged 35), a veteran of aerial combat in the Pacific during the Second World War, Carrier Air Group (CAG)-11, addressed the pilots prior to launch. Lieutenant Commander William T. Amen led VF-111's first launch, taking his men to sweep airfields at Mokpo, Kwangju and Kusan. VF-112's Panthers, two divisions of four aircraft, similarly hit targets in the Mokpo–Kwangju area. Vogel was KIA on 19 August during a strike against a bridge near Seoul. His formation of four Corsairs hit a bridge span with one 500-pounder on the first pass but on his second pass enemy AA fire hit his Corsair. The other pilots saw his chute stream, but it did not open and his body hurtled to the ground. Vogel left a widow and five children.

Roland H. Baker

An F4U-4 gets the 'GO' signal from the Flight Deck Officer aboard *Philippine Sea*. Of all the fighters built during the Second World War, the 'Bent Winged Bird' remained in production the longest. (After more than ten years in production, Vought stopped building Corsairs on Christmas Eve 1952.) Corsairs were one of several Second World War types still in front-line service at the outbreak of the Korean War, the first F4U-4Cs (armed with four 20 mm cannon in place of the six .50 inch machine guns of earlier versions) reaching the battle zone with USMC squadrons aboard *Sicily* and *Badoeing Strait*. In the first ten months of the Korean War, Corsairs flew 82 per cent of USN and USMC tactical support missions. While jets were about 100 mph faster than Corsairs or Skyraiders, the early jets could not haul as great a warload over a long distance, and they were slow to respond from when the throttle was advanced to the time the engine 'spooled up' sufficiently to accelerate the aircraft. This delay could prove fatal if a jet had to be waved off a landing at the last moment. Corsairs, with their huge variable-pitch propellers and water-injected R-2800 Double-Wasps, permitted fast acceleration.

Roland H. Baker

Opposite, above: Ordnancemen on board *Philippine Sea* bring out their bombs to load on the wings of the F4U-4s. CV-47 launched pre-invasion strikes in the Inchon–Seoul area on 12–14 September 1950, and furnished air cover for the Inchon landing on the 15th. In this bold thrust, the First Marine Division took the enemy by surprise, captured the port of Inchon and, with the Army's 7th Infantry Division, captured Seoul and Kimpo airfield, serving Communist supply routes to the south. Breaking the enemy stranglehold on Pusan, UN forces seized the initiative.

Roland H. Baker

Below: Napalm being prepared prior to a strike on North Korea. Napalm, or napalmgel, is a petrol thickened with a compound made from aluminium, naphthenic and palmitic acids, to which white phosphorous is added for ignition.

Roland H. Baker

A drop tank containing the deadly Napalm is manhandled into position on deck for loading aboard an F4U-4 Corsair. During nine months of operations, August 1950 to May 1951, CV-47 expended 5,985 tons of bombs and rockets, and 1,335 tons of Napalm.

Roland H. Baker

F4U-4s are launched from the deck of *Philippine Sea* and the strike begins.

Roland H. Baker

An F4U-4 leaves the forward deck of *Philippine Sea*. On 15 September 1950 General Douglas MacArthur launched Operation CHROMITE using amphibious landings behind the enemy lines at Inchon with the majority of the air cover provided by F4Us and Skyraiders from *Valley Forge, Philippine Sea* and *Boxer* (recently arrived from the USA). Fighter-bombers strafed and bombed positions along the Inchon waterfront prior to the main landing and by midnight the operation had achieved all the objectives. The North Koreans fell back in the face of the offensive and the Navy pilots went in search of interdiction targets. By 28 September the Communists were in full retreat and by 9 October American troops had crossed the 38th Parallel and were heading for Pyongyang, the North Korean capital.

Roland H. Baker

A Catapult Officer signals the launching of an F9F-2B of VF-111 from the deck of *Philippine Sea* on 21 September 1950. The Panther was to remain the Navy's first-line jet fighter throughout the first year of the Korean War. Of the 826 Navy and USMC jets deployed, no fewer than 715 were F9F-2s, and they flew about 78,000 combat sorties.

via Philip Jarrett

Philippine Sea's aircraft return, guided in by the Landing Signals Officer (LSO) or 'Paddles' as he is known. Between 16 September and 3 October 1950, CVG-11 furnished 'deep support' of allied forces and bombed supply routes and airfields from Seoul to Pyongyang. On 17 September Ensign Edward D. Jackson Jr. (aged 25) of VF-112, while pressing a low-level strafing run south of Seoul, flew through high-tension cables strung across the Han River. His F9F sustained extensive damage and he suffered painful facial lacerations and partial blindness. His wingman, Ensign Dayl E. Crow, 'talked' him to the ship and into the groove. The LSO took it from there and brought him safely on board in a blind landing, as Jackson caught the number five wire.

Roland H. Baker

A flight crewman ushers the Corsair away after landing. Roland H. Baker

Wings folded, a Corsair is placed below for the day. Tomorrow another strike will begin. Roland H. Baker

Roland H. 'Bake' Baker (left), Assistant Air Intelligence Officer on *Philippine Sea*, with fellow officers. Baker had flown Hellcats in the Pacific War during the Second World War and was recalled to active duty when the Korean War began.

Roland H. Baker

'Swede', a heavily bewhiskered sailor on board *Philippine Sea*.

Roland H. Baker

This signaller is wrapped up against the cold as he sends a message from his carrier to an escort in TF-77.

Roland H. Baker

An aircraft maintainer works on the engine of an F4U-4 on board *Philippine Sea*.

Roland H. Baker

Mount Fujiama forms a beautiful backdrop above the wing tip tanks of CV-47's Panthers, in harbour in Japan, and the USS *Sitkoh Bay* (CVE-86), a Casablanca Class escort carrier launched on 19 February 1944. (Korea resulted in the reactivation of Reserve Fleet carriers, five CVEs (and one CVL) being used in the conflict. CVE-86 was finally broken up in 1961.) *Philippine Sea* made seven replenishments at Sasebo and Yokosuka during the period August 1950 to May 1951, her first at Sasebo on 14/15 August 1950. CV-47 then returned to the east coast of Korea, commencing CAS for hard-pressed UN forces and bombing key bridges near Seoul on the 16th.

Roland H. Baker

An F9F-2 of VF-112 landing aboard USS *Philippine Sea*. In the background (to the left) is USS *Antietam* (CVS-36). The Panther was the first Navy jet to down another jet aircraft, when Lieutenant Commander William T. Amen, CAG VF-111 (flying a VF-112 F9F), destroyed a MiG-15 during a raid on bridges at Sinuiju on the Yalu on 9 November 1950. The month marked the massive intervention by Chinese Communist 'volunteers', who swarmed south to aid the North Koreans. The Chinese Air Force introduced a new element to the war – MiG-15s – which posed a serious threat to the prop-driven ADs and F4Us. On 26 November Red Chinese forces smashed into the 'greatly extended' UN forces in a surprise assault, driving a deep wedge between 8th Army and 10th Corps. The spectre of isolation and annihilation loomed large as Allied troops pulled back before the enemy onslaught.

Grumman

'Home by Christmas? No Way'. (Roland H. Baker is pictured on the left.) A crewman has made his displeasure known by writing 'Nuts' on the propeller of a frozen F4U-4. Between 2 and 25 December 1950 TF-77's planes conducted CAS in the Chosin Reservoir area, covering the successful extraction of ground forces (most notably the 1st Marine Division) to Hungnam and evacuation. Lieutenant (Junior Grade; jg) Thomas J. Hudner, of VF-32, flying from *Leyte* on 4 December 1950, was the only Corsair pilot awarded the Medal of Honor during the Korean War. Hudner deliberately made a wheels-up landing behind enemy lines to go to the aid of downed wingman Ensign Jesse L. Brown (the Navy's first black aviator), who was trapped in his burning F4U-4, but his valiant effort was in vain.

Roland H. Baker

Roland H. Baker in more equitable weather on board *Philippine Sea*.

Roland H. Baker

Between 26 March and 2 April 1951, at Okusuka, the *Philippine Sea* disembarked CVG-11 and embarked three F4U-4 Corsair squadrons: VF-24 ('405', a yellow-tipped VF-24 aircraft is pictured); VF-63; and VF-64. VA-65's Skyraiders and the usual Composite Squadron detachments – all from CVG-2 – which previously had served on board *Valley Forge* also embarked.

Roland H. Baker

A pair of F9F-2 Panthers of VF-191 (B) and a F9F-5P Photo Panther of VC-61 (PP) circle for a landing back aboard USS *Princeton*, or 'The Sweet Pea' as it was nicknamed by her crew, after completing an air strike on enemy troop concentrations and ammunition dumps, 16 July 1951.

Grumman

An F9F-5, piloted by Ensign Pyle of VF-781, heads for the barrier aboard USS *Oriskany* (CV-34) on 29 March 1951.

USN

An F9F-2B fighter-bomber of VF-721, a Glenview, Illinois, reserve unit embarked aboard USS *Boxer* in August 1951. Demobilization following the Second World War had severely reduced the fighting capability of the US forces and no fewer than twenty-eight Navy and Marine Reserve squadrons were called to active duty from July to September 1950. In all, eighteen Reserve squadrons made twenty-nine deployments on board carriers during the Korean War.

Grumman

In August 1951 USS *Essex* (CV-9) arrived on station joining TF-77, and its McDonnell F2H-2 Banshees made their combat debut on 23 August, with VF-172, flying an escort mission for the B-29s. Pictured aboard *Essex*, in Korean waters in August 1951, the F2H-2s are serviced prior to strikes against Communist-held sectors on the Asiatic mainland. A naval airman rides the starboard wing tank of a Banshee while fuelling the aircraft for one of its first combat missions in Korea.

USN

A naval airman fuses and secures the arming wire on a bomb mounted below the wing of a VF-172 'Banjo' destined for Communist forces ashore.

USN

Lieutenant Dauphin climbs into the cockpit of F2H-2 Banshee BuNo124974, aboard CV-9 in Korean waters, October 1951, while crewmen swarm over the 'Banjo' making last-minute preparations for flight. Guns are being checked, the nose-wheel dolly disconnected, screens have been removed, and all external points noted on the check list.

McDonnell Corp

Skyraiders and VF-713's F4U Corsairs on board USS *Antietam* (CVS-36) off Korea on 15 October 1951.

USN

As a matter of some urgency – the USN desperately needed to achieve performance parity with the MiG-15 – swept wings and tail were added to the standard Grumman Panther fuselage and the F9F-6 Cougar was born in 1951. The first of two prototypes flew on 20 September that year. Beginning in November 1951, VF-32 became the first fleet squadron to convert to the Cougar. Soon, F9F-6s and -7s re-equipped some twenty USN fighter squadrons.

Grumman

Fuselage gleaming in the sunlight, a MAC Banshee of VF-172 streaks past the coastline on its way back to the carrier USS *Essex* after a combat mission over enemy territory. Banshees were sent on varying missions, striking at rail lines and bridges as well as escorting B-29 Superfortresses on bombing raids. Late in 1951 two future astronauts made the headlines. On 23 October Lieutenant Walter M. Schirra, USN, shot down a MiG while on an exchange with the 136th FB Wing. On a later mission, Ensign Neil A. Armstrong, from *Essex*, baled out and was rescued after his Panther was hit during a strafing run near Wonsan.

USN

On the flight deck of USS *Antietam* in the Sea of Japan off the coast of Korea on 12 January 1952 an F9F-2 of VF-831, a reserve squadron called to active duty during the Korean crisis, is readied by aircrewmen for another strike. It is armed with four standard 5 inch HVARS and two 6.5 inch diameter anti-tank (ATAR) 'Ram rockets'. The warhead on the standard 5 inch HVAR was found to be too small to penetrate the Soviet-built T-34 tanks used by North Korea and the 6.5 inch rocket was airlifted to Korea as an emergency measure.

Grumman

USS *Ranier* (AE-5) pulling away after replenishing USS *Antietam* (CV-36) and USS *Wisconsin* (BB-64) in Korean waters, February 1952. In early March 1952 TF-77 was part of Operation SATURATE, a sustained offensive aimed at short sections of railway line to deny their use to the enemy. By April, TF-77 comprised: *Valley Forge* with Air Task Group 1 (ATG-1) (VF-52/111/194/653 and four detachments) embarked; *Philippine Sea* (which, after an overhaul, had rejoined TF-77 on 3 February) with ATG-11 (VF-112/113/114/115 and four detachments); *Boxer* with ATG-2 (VF-24/63/64/65 and three detachments); and *Princeton* with ATG-19 (VF-191/192/193/195 and four detachments). (At the end of the war *Lake Champlain* was on station in place of *Valley Forge*.)

USN

A photo unit Fox McDonnell F2H-2P over a devastated North Korean target area, April 1952. The F2H-2P reconnaissance prototype, a modified F2H-2, first flew on 12 October 1950. Eighty-eight unarmed F2H-2Ps, which mounted six cameras in an elongated nose, were built, the last being delivered on 28 May 1952.

McDonnell

On 23 June 1952, for the first time in eighteen months, four Fleet Carriers – *Philippine Sea*, *Bon Homme Richard*, *Boxer* (CV-21; pictured), and *Princeton* (CV-37) – were operating together off the Korean coast. At 1400 hours on 23 June the four carriers commenced launching the biggest strike of the war at the time, against the hitherto untouched hydro-electric plant at Suiho, a major source of power for Manchurian industry. Altogether, thirty-five Skyraiders from *Boxer*'s VA-65, *Princeton*'s VA-195 and *Philippine Sea*'s VA-115 took part.

Roland H. Baker

An F4U-4 of VF-24, with empty weapons racks and wings folded upwards, taxies down the flight deck of *Philippine Sea* after another strike over Korea. On 11 July 1952 TF-77 took part in Operation PRESSURE PUMP, the largest air attack so far, against thirty military targets in Pyongyang. Some 1,254 sorties were flown for the loss of just three aircraft. On 29 August an even mightier force, including USMC Panthers and F4Us and Navy Corsairs, Banshees and Panthers from *Boxer* and *Essex*, returned to devastate the capital. On 1 September 1952 TF-77 despatched the largest naval air strike of the war when aircraft from *Essex, Princeton* and *Bon Homme Richard* left the synthetic oil refinery at Aoji in ruins.

Roland H. Baker

An F4U-4 Corsair of VF-24 is placed on the lift below the deck of *Philippine Sea*.

Roland H. Baker

F9F-2 Panthers of VF-721 head toward their target.

An F9F-5P Photo Panther of VC-81 and two F9F-2s of VF-72 head back to *Bon Homme Richard* after a strike in North Korea, 19 December 1952.

An F-9F2B Panther from VF-72 aboard USS *Bon Homme Richard* firing rocket projectiles against a North Korean target.

USN

A North American AJ-2P Savage (easily distinguishable by its bulbous camera nose), one of thirty reconnaissance models built, and which equipped two shore-based photographic squadrons, pictured at either Itazuke or Haneda AFB, Japan, at the time of the Korean War. Captain Paul F. Stevens remembers: 'The Navy had to develop an atomic bomb delivery system quickly. It submitted dimensions required for the bomb bay and told the contractor to build an airplane around it – and hurry!' The first of three XAJ-1 prototypes, ordered on 24 June 1946, was flown on 3 July 1948. The first of fifty-five AJ-1s, begun in June 1947, flew on 10 May 1949, and the AJ-2P flew for the first time on 30 March 1952. All were powered by a combination of two Pratt & Whitney R-2800-44W Wasps and an Allison J33-A-10 turbojet in the fuselage. AJ-1s entered service in September 1949 with VC-5, which made the first Savage take-off from *Coral Sea* on 21 April 1950.

USN

THE LAST A J

AND THE JACKASS

WHO FLEW IT

DANGER→ PROPELL

The 'Last AJ', at Port Lyautey, French Morocco, by pilots of VC-7. Captain Paul F. Stevens remembers: 'The early Savage was unreliable, required a high level of maintenance and experienced many accidents. Fundamentally, it was a very complex airplane and consequently the systems failed often (several gallons of hydraulic fluid were always carried). The cowling on the engines was very tight and overheated while climbing for altitude regularly. Fire warning red lights were on and off routinely and did not contribute to the pilot's comfort. The radar bombing system was a bear to maintain. The two R-2800 P&W engines were turbo-super-charged so one could pull full power all the way up to 40,000 ft. At high altitudes the J-33 jet engine carried a good deal of the load. The AJ-1 would do 400 knots, carried a nuclear bomb, and had an all-weather capability. Flying it on and off the straight carrier deck day and night was a fright. It was not very comfortable knowing that a barrier had never stopped an AJ-1 when missing an arresting wire, and the AJ-1s were always recovered last. Looking at the pack of airplanes forward of the barrier made one work hard to make an "OK" pass.' Fifty-five standard AJ-2s, first flown on 18 February 1953, were built. The Savage equipped eight heavy-attack squadrons and remained in production until June 1954.

via Captain Paul F. Stevens USN (Retd)

A Martin PBM-5A Mariner, one of thirty-six PBM-5A amphibious models with retractable tricycle gear built between April 1948 and March 1949, at either Itazuke or Haneda AFB, Japan, during the Korean War. Production of the PBM-5 followed the PBM-3D, some 592 of the former being built in 1944/45. By June 1947, 629 PBM-5s had been completed, some modified to PBM-5E with APS-15 radar. Altogether, 1,366 Mariners were built, some serving the USN until July 1958.

USN

A Sikorsky H03S-1 of Helicopter Utility Squadron One (HU-1) at either Itazuke or Haneda AFB, Japan, at the time of the Korean War. At sea each carrier had a single H03S-1 (UP-29) of HU-1 for plane guard and utility duties. HU-1 helicopters were nicknamed 'Angels' for their role as ASR aircraft for downed pilots.

USN

Two-seat Grumman F7F-3N night-fighter somersaults after landing on the deck of USS *Philippine Sea* during the Korean War. Production of the F7F Tigercat had ended in November 1946 but the type was still in service at the time of the Korean War, predominantly with the USMC, which regarded the Tigercat highly. The same could not be said of the USN, who had misgivings about using the 'hot' fighter on board carriers. The F7F-3N's long nose housed the SCR-70 radar but the .50 inch guns as mounted in the nose of the F7F-3 single-seat version were deleted. Altogether, 250 F7F-3 fighters/-3N/single-seat -3P reconnaissance models were built for the USN and USMC, bringing total Tigercat production to 364. The appearance of MiG-15 jets led to the Tigercats being withdrawn from service in 1952.

Grumman

Forty-five F4U-5N night-fighters were built with an APS-19 radar intercept scanner in a housing on the starboard wing. F4U-5NL was the designation given to seventy-two 'winterized' night-fighters identical to the F4U-5N except for modification carried out for its use in Korea. Several F4U-5Ns were subsequently brought up to the same standard. In July 1953 Lieutenant Guy P. Bordelon Jr. and a fellow F4U-5N pilot of VC-3 (the Navy's only all-weather combat fighter squadron), aboard USS *Princeton*, were despatched to K-6 airfield south of Seoul to try to counter 'Heckling' missions flown by NKAF Yak-18 training aircraft, which were proving more than just a nuisance to USMC operations. (On the night of 16/17 July a NKAF Yak-18 bombed a fuel dump at Inchon, destroying 5 million gallons of fuel.) In three night missions over a three-week period Bordelon destroyed five 'Bed Check Charlies', as they were known, to become the only Navy ace in Korea. Apart from night air-superiority sorties, F4U-5Ns often guided Skyraiders to their targets, dropping flares and leading the attack. VC-3 detachments served aboard nine of the twelve carriers that operated off Korea. The last Corsairs were taken out of USN first-line service in December 1954, while VBF-4, relegated to the Reserve, served until 1957.

USN

Opposite, above: A VC-61 photo unit Fox F2H-2P reconnaissance Banshee and VF-11 'Red Ripper' F2H 'Banjo' escort from USS *Kearsarge* cross the North Korean coast, April 1953. While F2Hs formed part of the Reserve strength until 1965, the operational life of the F2H-2Ps was prolonged until suitable replacements could be found.

McDonnell

Below: Underway Replenishment (UNREP) taking place between USS *Virgo* (AKA-20) and USS *Lake Champlain* (CVA-39) en route to Japan, 8 June 1953, when carrier-borne aircraft flew ground-support missions for seven days. On 14/15 June TF-77, comprising *Boxer*, *Philippine Sea*, *Princeton* and *Lake Champlain*, flew round-the-clock missions in support of the First Republic of Korea Corps' attacks to regain 'Anchor Hill'.

USN

F9Fs, ADs and F4Us warming up on the deck of USS *Bon Homme Richard* (CVA-31) for another strike against the Communists in Korea on Thanksgiving Day, 27 November 1952.

USN

Opposite, above: By the end of the Korean War the number of carriers of all types had risen to thirty-four (from just fifteen at the start of the war). During *Philippine Sea*'s last deployment, 31 January to 27 July 1953 (the day of the Armistice), she launched 7,243 sorties and logged just over 7,700 traps. The Communists signed the Armistice on 27 July and the 38-month war was over. CVA-47 (pictured) reached Alameda, California, on 14 August 1953. Only twelve years old, *Philippine Sea* was placed out of commission, in reserve, on 22 December 1958 and she became an 'auxiliary aircraft carrier transport' in May 1959 before being stricken on 1 December 1969 and sold for scrap in 1971.

Roland H. Baker

Below: F9F-5 Panther jets wait to take off from the deck of *Antietam* (CV-36) near Portsmouth, England, on 1 July 1953 as a Douglas Sky Knight becomes airborne from the carrier. The Allison A33-A16 used on the F9F-4 was replaced by a Pratt & Whitney J48-P-2 (modelled on the Rolls-Royce Tay) on the F9F-5, which differed from previous models as it had a higher pointed tail. By December 1952, 619 F9F-5s had been accepted. The clear-coated natural metal finish adopted by the Panthers in this picture was experimental and proved to be unsatisfactory in the salt sea air and was soon discontinued.

via Philip Jarrett

The USN received thirty-six
Convair R4Y-1s (Model 340-71)
between 1 August 1955 and 27
June 1956 (BuNo140993 is
pictured). Most were converted
to 440 standard and
redesignated C-131F in 1962.
One was converted for
Electronic Counter Measures
(ECM) training as an EC-131G
and others were modified to
VC-131Fs.

Convair

As AD-6 BuNo128959 of VA-65 approached USS *Yorktown* at the end of its sortie, December 1953, the tailhook failed to extend and the Skyraider took the barrier and nosed over. As the propeller dug into the deck, one of the blades broke off.

USN

The USN became the first military customer for the Super Constellation on 14 July 1950 when it placed an order for six PO-2W AEW aircraft, to be followed by orders for 202 more versions. Super Connies were operated by the USN (and USAF) for twenty-six years, from November 1952 to October 1978.

Lockheed

The USN obtained 142 WV-2 AEW aircraft, which were redesignated EC-121K in September 1962 under a new military service designation system.

Lockheed

The Grumman XF10F-1 Jaguar was the world's first variable-sweep fighter but development was so protracted that only one was ever completed. Here, test pilot Corwin H. 'Corky' Meyer is about to take the Westinghouse XJ40-powered XF10F-1 up on its first test flight, at Edwards AFB, on 19 May 1952. The wing sweep mechanism worked perfectly but the first flight revealed problems with the flaps, trim and flap controls, and rudder buffet. Her second flight two days later ended with Meyer having to land with a dead stick because of a defective fuel control unit. Subsequent tests produced more airframe and engine deficiencies, and finally, on 1 April 1953, the USN cancelled production contracts.

Grumman

Opposite, above: Four Lockheed R7V-2 (Model 1249A-95-75) transport versions of the Super Constellation were obtained by the USN. The first aircraft flew on 1 September 1954.

Lockheed

Below: The WV-2E airborne electronic testbed (BuNo126512), the first AEW aircraft to be fitted with a rotodome (containing antenna for the APS-82 radar), first flew on 8 August 1956. In 1962 the WV-2E was redesignated EC-121L-LO.

Lockheed

When the Korean War ended there were twenty-four Navy Skyraider squadrons. By September 1955 this had risen to twenty-nine, and three versions of the AD-5 (pictured above) and AD-6 ground-support single-seater aircraft (AD-6 of VA-45, pictured opposite, above) were in production (all told, no less than twenty-two versions of the Skyraider were built). A USN hunter-killer team comprised an AD-5 hunter and AD-6 killer. The four-seat AD-5W (218 built) was an AEW aircraft fitted with a ventral APS-20 'guppy' radome for over-the-horizon detection. Two radar operators were carried within the fuselage, necessitating the removal of dive-brakes. An experimental clear-coated natural metal finish with black codes was applied to selected aircraft within certain squadrons and was in use from 29 April 1952 to 16 February 1955, when it was cancelled because of problems with corrosion. Under the 1962 Tri-Service designation system, the 'Able-Dog' 5W became the EA-1E (pictured opposite, below).

Douglas

In 1947/48 fifty F-80Cs were transferred to the USN (and USMC) as TO-1s (TV-1s after 1950). The USN received 699 TV-1/T2V-1 Sea-Stars (the first twenty-eight being designed TO-2s), carrier-based versions of the T-33B-LO. The T-33B (TV-2) was a two-seat Navy trainer version of the successful F-80 series aircraft. It had a fuselage lengthened by 3 ft, leading-edge slats fitted to the wing and a larger tail surface. Between 1956 and 1958 Lockheed built 150 TV-1/T2V-1 Sea-Stars, a carrier-based version of the T-33, for the USN.

Lockheed

The delta-winged Douglas XF4D-1 Skyray (BuNo124586), which first flew on 23 January 1951, should have been powered by a Westinghouse XJ40 engine, but this was still being developed and a 5,000 lb thrust Allison J35-A-17 turbojet was fitted instead. In September 1953 the Hawker Hunter 3 recaptured the air speed record for Britain and then the Supermarine Swift 4 increased it to 735.70 mph. BuNo124587, the second prototype Skyray, fitted with the 11,600 lb thrust XJ40-WE-8B afterburning engine, was put forward, and on 3 October 35-year-old Second World War and Korean War Veteran Lieutenant Commander James B. Verdin, USN, took off in the second XF4D-1 prototype from El Centro Naval Base, 40 miles from the Mojave Desert, and headed for the Salton Sea 3 km (1.86 mile) course. Verdin made four passes and set a new world speed record with an average speed of 752.94 mph (this stood until 28 August 1961 when it was eclipsed by the F4H Phantom).

Douglas

During 1951 the two XF4D-1 prototypes tried the Westinghouse XJ40-WE-6 and WE-8, but failure of this engine programme led to the new Pratt & Whitney J57-P-2 being adopted for the first series production and it was five years before the first F4D-1 short-range interceptors entered squadron service, on 16 April 1956, with Composite Squadron (VC-3) at Moffett Field, California. (Later, as VF(AW)-3, the squadron became the only Navy squadron assigned to USAF Air Defence Command (ADC).) Known in service as the 'ten minute killer' (because of its rapid climb to interception altitude) or 'Ford', the F4D-1 Skyray eventually equipped eleven first-line USN squadrons. It was armed with four 20 mm cannon and six external hard points could carry 4,000 lb of bombs, rockets or other external stores, including a fuel tank with a refuelling probe. The 419th and last F4D-1 (230 others were cancelled) was delivered on 22 December 1958. F4C-1 (F-6A from September 1962) Skyrays served until 1964.

McDonnell Douglas

Lockheed P2V-5F (P-2E) Neptune BuNo124892 of VW-3. Markings for five hurricane-hunting missions are painted beneath the cockpit. The P2V-5 first flew on 29 December 1950 and 424 examples were built under six sub-model designations, making it the most numerous of all Neptune models. In addition to two 3,500 hp R-3350-32W Turbo Compound engines, the -5F was boosted by two 3,250 lb thrust Westinghouse J34-WE-34 turbojets in underslung wing pods to increase take-off power and dash speed.

Lockheed via GMS

P2V-7 BuNo140964 with MAD system 'stinger' tail (as first introduced on the P2V-5), twin .50 calibre guns in a dorsal turret, smaller ventral radome, and tip tanks. The YP2V-7 prototype flew on 26 April 1954. The P2V-7 was the final production version of the Neptune, some 287 (including forty-eight assembled by Kawasaki in Japan) being built under three sub-model designations by 1962. Some P2V-7/P-2Hs were later converted to P2V-7S/SP-2H and other variants.

Lockheed

The Lockheed XFV-1 was designed to rise vertically, level off for swift, horizontal flight, and land on its tail wheels by hanging suspended by contra-rotating propellers geared to a single Allison XT-40-A (twin T38 turbine) engine. The XFV-1 first flew on 16 June 1954. The research programme was concluded in 1955 after providing much valuable data for military consideration on VTOL aircraft.

Lockheed

F2H-3 Banshee all-weather fighters being parked on the flight deck of USS *Hornet* (CVA-12) during operations with the US Seventh Fleet in the Far East, 1 October 1954. An order for 250 F2H-3s was placed on 14 July 1950 (thirty-nine being given to the Royal Canadian Navy) and the first flew on 29 March 1952. The aircraft was initially accepted in June 1952 and the last was delivered on 24 September 1953. F2H-3s had a redesigned tail complex, APQ-41 radar in the nose, carried more fuel than previous models, and had droppable tip tanks, four 20 mm cannon, with 600 rounds, two pylons for 500 lb bombs, and eight for 250 lb bombs or rockets. The 150 F2H-4s were similar but had APG-37 radar. Banshees were last delivered on 30 October 1953 and finally retired from USN first-line fighter squadrons after September 1959.

USN

Winner of an ASW competition in June 1950, the Grumman XS2F-1 (design G-89) first flew on 4 December 1952. It was the first aircraft design to combine the detection equipment and armament to hunt and destroy submarines, as well as operate from an aircraft carrier. Production deliveries began in 1953, and in 1954 the S2F-1 was the first aircraft to be launched by the new steam catapult from the deck of an American carrier, USS *Hancock*. Some 1,369 Trackers were produced in sixteen different configurations, including 100 CS2F-1s and -2s built under licence. Pictured is S2F-1 (S-2A) Tracker BuNo147531, one of 740 built by Grumman for ASW service at sea.

Grumman via GMS

In 1953 Vought began building the F7U-1 Cutlass at a new plant at Dallas, Texas. The design was radical, having a cantilever mid-mounted trapezoid wing, swept at an angle of 38 degrees with slats along the entire span of the leading-edge (lateral control was by elevons, which handled the functions of both elevators and ailerons). The first XF7U-1, with two Westinghouse J34-WE-22 engines, flew on 29 September 1948 but lost power. Test pilot J. Robert Baker got the aircraft down safely but was killed a few weeks later in the same aircraft when it went out of control and crashed. Four more XF7U-1/early F7U-1s crashed during 1948–50, killing two other test pilots (another was killed in 1952). Only fourteen F7U-1s were produced, and the planned order for eighty-eight F7U-2s, which were to have been powered by the J34-WE-42, was cancelled. The first of the 192 F7U-3s did not reach the fleet until 1954 (with VC-3), the first sixteen being powered by Allison J35-A-29s, the rest by Westinghouse J46-WE-8As. Pictured are four F7U-3 Cutlasses from VF-124 at NAS Miramar over the Pacific coastline at San Diego, California, in March 1955.

USN via Philip Jarrett

Opposite, above: An F7U-3 Cutlass shooting flame from its afterburners as it roars off the steam catapult aboard USS *Hancock* during launching, March 1955.

USN via Philip Jarrett

Below: During 1954/55 ninety-eight F7U-3Ms (the USN's first fighter to carry four Sparrow I AAMs) were produced. Pictured is a -3M with a camera/rocket pack. The first F7U-3Ms were delivered to VF-124 and VF-81 in 1954. The last Cutlasses were withdrawn from service in November 1957.

Vought via Philip Jarrett

Pictured from on board
an F7U-3P Cutlass are
F7U-3s from VX-3 at
NAS Atlantic City, New
Jersey, in formation flight
over Pennsylvania, late
1955. Twelve F7U-3P
PR models were built.

Vought via Philip Jarrett

The McDonnell Model 58/XF3H-1, powered by a 7,200 lb thrust Westinghouse J40-WE-6 turbojet, flew on 7 August 1951. F3H-1N Demon night-fighters were to have increased fuel and improved radar for all-weather capability, which meant an increase in weight from 22,000 to 29,000 lb, but a more powerful J40-WE-24 was expected to compensate for this increase. However, this engine never materialized and they were powered by the J40-WE-22. The first F3H-1N (BuNo133489, pictured) flew on 24 December 1953. The Demon programme was dogged by a series of fatal accidents, caused mainly by persistent engine failures. The first XF3H-1 was lost in flight on 18 March 1954 when the engine exploded, and the second prototype was permanently grounded. Six F3H-1Ns were lost in eleven accidents killing three more pilots, and only fifty-eight of the planned 150 F3H-1Ns were produced. None were put into service, being used instead as ground trainers or simply scrapped. In 1955 the J40-WE-22 was replaced by the more powerful Allison J71-A-2 on the F3H-2 all-weather, fighter-bomber version, the first flying on 23 April 1955.

McDonnell via Philip Jarrett

Opposite, above: Of the 1,000 F3H Demons originally forecast, 519 production models were built. Some 142 F3H-2Ns (the first entering service with VF-14 in March 1956) were followed by eighty F3H-2Ms armed with four AIM-7 Sparrow III missiles. The final variant was the F3H-2 (239 of which were built), which could carry up to 6,000 lb of conventional stores including four Sparrow AIM-7Cs or four AIM-9B Sidewinders. Pictured are F3H-2s BuNo145242 and 1453412 of VF-131 from USS *Constellation* (CVA-64), 19 March 1962. At one time, eleven Navy squadrons were equipped with the Demon. The last F3H-2Ns were phased out during September 1964.

USN via Philip Jarrett

Opposite, below: The prototype single-seat Vought XF8U-1 Crusader flew on 25 March 1955 and VF-32 'Swordsmen' was the first squadron to receive the F8U-1 (F-8A) in March 1957, which then joined USS *Saratoga* in February 1958. No. '202' of VF-32 is pictured here on board 'Sara Maru' or 'Super Sara' (as it is known).

Vought via Philip Jarrett

In front of a curtain of steam coming from USS *Saratoga*'s angled-deck port catapult, F8U-1 '206' of VF-32 is positioned for launching. Until the appearance of the F-14A Tomcat in 1973, the F8U-1 (F-8A) Crusader was the 'last of the gunfighters', probably the finest pure fighter of the jet age and the Navy's first aircraft capable of more than 1,000 mph. It was also the world's first variable-incidence jet fighter (to eliminate an exaggerated nose-up tendency during landing).

Vought via Philip Jarrett

Opposite, above: Two F8U-1 Crusaders from VF-142 are caught in aerial formation over NAS Miramar, California, where the unit was stationed. VF-142 was one of the first West Coast squadrons to receive the new supersonic Navy fighter.

USN via Philip Jarrett

Below: F8U-1P Crusaders of VFP-61 from NAS Mirimar, California, the first West Coast squadron to receive the long-range photo Crusaders. The F8U-1P first flew on 17 December 1956, and Major John Glenn flew one from Los Angeles to New York in 3 hours 22 minutes on 16 July 1957; the first supersonic transcontinental flight. A total of 144 F8U-1Ps were accepted by March 1960.

Vought via Philip Jarrett

F8U Crusaders of VF-103 from USS *Forrestal* (CVA-59) over the Mediterranean on 26 July 1960. F8Us began to come off the production lines in January 1959 and by September 1960, 187 had been built. The F8U-2N night-fighter version had a more powerful engine, new avionics, autopilot, and infra-red ray screen.

USN via Philip Jarrett

Lieutenant (jg) J. Kryway has good reason to thank his Martin-Baker Mk.5 ejection seat as his burning F8 Crusader crashes off the flight deck of USS *Franklin D. Roosevelt* on 21 October 1961. By the early 1950s the survival rate in the USN (which used US-designed and built seats) for ejections below 1,000 ft was only 4 per cent; between 1,000 and 2,000 ft it was less than 50 per cent; and between 2,000 and 3,000 ft it was 66 per cent (256 men were killed during 1956/57 alone). On 28 August 1957 Martin-Baker successfully demonstrated its Mk.4 ejection seat at the USN test facility at Patuxent River, Maryland, when Flight Lieutenant Sydney Hughes RAF ejected from the aft cockpit of an F9F-8T Cougar flying at ground level at 120 mph. The USN finally decided to standardize Martin-Baker seats for all USN jet fighters and trainers. The Mk.5 seat was introduced in 1957 and the American system of jettisoning the canopy was linked up with the face blind firing handle. In 1965, following another successful demonstration at China Lake, the USN decided to fit Martin-Baker rocket seats in the Crusader, Intruder, and Phantom aircraft by modifying the Mk.5 seats already in service.

via Philip Jarrett

Douglas was awarded a two-prototype contract on 31 March 1949 for the XA3D-1 two-jet bomber, created by Ed Heinemann's design team and the largest and heaviest aircraft capable of carrier operation (it weighed 35 tons at take-off). The XA3D-1 first flew on 28 October 1952 with XJ40–WE-3 engines. Some forty-nine first production A3D-1s (A-3A after 1962) fitted with Pratt & Whitney J57-P-6 engines were built. A Mk.15 nuclear bomb, six 1,600 lb bombs, or six Mk.36 mines could be delivered on a target 1,150 miles distant at 621 mph top speed. (Pictured is A3D-1 BuNo135440. Note the Westinghouse radar-controlled tail turret containing twin 20 mm cannon and 1,000 rounds.) Heavy Attack Squadron One (VAH-1), commanded by Paul F. Stevens, was the first fleet squadron to receive the Skywarrior, on 31 March 1956, at NAS Jacksonville, Florida. He recalls: 'The A3D was in great demand for fleet participation during the whole year – a new and tremendous addition to the Fleet's striking capabilities. At that time our attack altitude was 50,000'. We were rarely intercepted by the opposing fighters. Bringing this big bird aboard required more piloting skills than any other modern airplane. However, the flying qualities were very good but the margins for error were very thin. The A3D had the great P&W J-57, the first of the highly reliable and excellent fuel/thrust specifics. The A3D was much, much lighter than the RB-66 and was designed for PERFORMANCE. It had no ejection seat, a sacrifice to obtain altitude and cruise efficiencies but well worth it.'

Douglas

Opposite, above: BuNo148321 *The Crown*, a ski- and JATO-equipped (Jet Assisted Take-Off) LC-130F of VX-6, blasts off a snowfield in Antarctica. This aircraft was delivered in August 1960 and it made its first flight into the Antarctic during the winter season of 1962. *The Crown* crashed during take-off 1200 km from McMurdo on 15 January 1975 when a JATO bottle broke loose, and it sank into the ice. The aircraft was freed from the ice in December 1986, temporarily repaired, and flown out in January 1988 to Christchurch, New Zealand, for permanent repair. After ten more years' service with VX-6/VXE-6, *The Crown* was withdrawn in 1999.

Lockheed

Below: Grumman's much improved F9F-8 Cougar differed from previous F9F series aircraft as it had a more powerful engine, an air-refuelling probe in the nose of a longer fuselage, and longer range. The first F9F-8 flew on 18 December 1953 and the aircraft was first deployed overseas in July 1956 with VA-46. It was the first fighter capable of operational use of the AIM Sidewinder air-to-air heat-seeking missile.

Grumman

The Douglas A-4 (A4D) Skyhawk was conceived in 1952 as a jet-powered successor to the AD-1 Skyraider, the XA4D-1 flying for the first time on 22 June 1954. Deliveries of A4D-1s to the USN began in September 1956. Pictured are Skyhawks of VA-126.

Douglas via GMS

Grumman TF-1 (C-1A) Trader BuNo136766, one of eighty-three Carrier Onboard Delivery (COD) aircraft built to replace the TBM-3R COD for transporting personnel, mail, and/or small-sized priority cargo to and from carriers. In its original form, with a crew of two, the TF-1 could accommodate either nine passengers or 3,500 lb of cargo, and finally, in 1953, after the rear door layout had been revised, it could even carry a 8,500 lb Mk.6 nuclear weapon. The 236th Tracker airframe was used as the first Trader, which flew on 19 January 1955. TF-1s began to enter USN service in October 1955. During the Vietnam War Traders shuttled personnel, mail and urgently needed supplies from shore bases to carriers. The last C-1As were withdrawn from first-line service in 1986.

Grumman

The first 123 A3D-2 (A-3B) Skywarriors built (BuNo153413 is pictured) differed from the A3D-1 as they had a strengthened airframe and were powered by the more powerful 10,500 lb thrust J57-P-10 engines. The next twenty were fitted with an air-refuelling probe. A3D-2s, which could carry an auxiliary fuel tank and two Mk.28 nuclear weapons in the bomb bay, first entered service with VAH-2 in 1957 and the Skywarrior squadrons became part of the overall nuclear deterrent force. Thirty RA-3B (A3D-2P) photographic reconnaissance versions of the hugely successful Skywarrior series were built. The first A3D-2 flew on 22 July 1958. A total of 283 Skywarriors were built, the last A-3Bs being delivered between April 1960 and January 1961.

Douglas

The Sixth Fleet, led by USS *Saratoga* (with Skywarriors, A-4 Skyhawks and McDonnell Demons embarked) and followed by USS *Essex*, a heavy cruiser and destroyers, passes through the Straits of Messina, 28 October 1959.

USN via Captain Paul F. Stevens USN (Retd

R4D-5L (LC-47H) BuNo12418, flown by Lieutenant Commander Conrad Shinn, takes off from the South Pole campsite for McMurdo Sound, Antarctica, 21 November 1956.

Douglas

R4D-5 BuNo12438 at NAS Miramar. Many R4D-5s were modified for a variety of special duties including air-sea warfare training, navigation training, Radio Counter Measures (RCM) and personnel transport.

Douglas

Four F9F-8s refuelling from a Convair R3Y-2 Tradewind. Some 602 F9F-8s were delivered between 29 February 1954 and 22 March 1957, and the majority were converted to F9F-8Bs with a Low Altitude Bombing System (LABS) nuclear-delivery capability. F9F-8Bs were finally phased out in 1958/59. Among the last Cougars were 110 F9F-8Ps fitted with seven cameras (delivered between August 1955 and July 1957), and these served photographic squadrons until February 1960. F9-8Ps were the last Cougars to serve a fleet squadron, being retained by VFP-62 until February 1960.

Grumman

Another Cougar model, the two-seat F9F-8T (TF-9J) trainer version, served from 1956 to 1974 and was responsible for training most of the pilots who flew combat missions in South-east Asia. Pictured is F9F-8T BuNo142470/No. 7 of the 'Blue Angels', who, after transitioning from F9F-5s to F9F-6s in 1953, were forced to re-equip briefly with Panthers as the fleet needed Cougars for operational squadrons. The 'Blues' finally exchanged their F9F-5s for F9F-8s in 1954 and operated the Cougar until converting to the F11F-1 at the end of the 1957 season. After converting to Tigers, the 'Blue Angels' still retained F9F-8T BuNo142470 and disposed of this aircraft only when the flight demonstration team re-equipped with F-4s in 1969.

Grumman

The F11F-1 (F-11A) Tiger, the Navy's first carrier-based supersonic fighter, was originally designated F9F-9 (for the first six aircraft) as a Cougar variant. BuNo138604 was the first of two short-nosed flying prototypes completed in July 1954 and was used in the initial trials at the new Peconic River facility at Calverton. Although it was only powered by a non-afterburning 7,500 lb Wright J65-W-7 turbojet (because the Americanized British Sapphire engine was not then available), Corwin 'Corky' Meyer almost reached Mach 1 on the first flight on 30 July. This aircraft crashed near Peconic River on 20 October after an engine flame-out and was so badly damaged that it was not rebuilt. The pilot, Lieutenant Commander W.H. Livingstone, survived.

Grumman via GMS

F9F-6 (F11F) BuNo138622, one of forty-two Service test and initial production aircraft (138606/647), armed with four Sidewinders.

Grumman

Deliveries of production F11F-1 Tigers powered by the J65-W18 with afterburner began with an assignment to VA-156, a combined fighter-attack squadron, at NAS Moffett Field, California, on 8 March 1957. Starting with BuNo141728, all F11F-1s were fitted with a longer nose and had the refuelling probe relocated to the starboard side of the nose cone to permit the installation of AN/APS-50 radar (which was never actually installed). Pictured in echelon formation are twelve F11F-1s o

VF-21, one of the two Atlantic Fleet squadrons that flew Tigers (the other being VF-33, which, with VF-111, was the last of the Fleet squadrons to operate F11F-1s in April 1961). The Tiger also equipped five Pacific Fleet squadrons.

Grumman

F9F-6 Bu1386124 inflight refuelling (with a production F11F-1 nose probe) from a Naval Air Training Center (NATC) North American A-2A tanker. In 1955 the A-2 was equipped with a tanker package that consisted of a fuel tank which filled the entire bomb bay, and a hose and reel system.

Grumman

An F11F-1 from the NATC Patuxent River, launching from *Saratoga*. The first catapult launchings and arrested landings were carried out during carrier suitability trials on board *Forrestal* on 4 April 1956. F11F-1s served on short detachments aboard *Bon Homme Richard*, *Forrestal*, *Intrepid* and *Ranger*, as well as the 'Super Sara'.

Grumman

Tiger production continued through December 1958, the last of 201 F11F-1s produced being delivered on 23 January 1959 (four F11F-1s of VF-21 are pictured). None of the planned PR versions were built, and only two F11F-1F 'Super Tigers' – faster than the F11F-1 but too heavy for carrier operations – were test flown. The F11F equipped the 'Blue Angels' flight demonstration team for a period longer than any other aircraft. Starting April 1957, they operated the short-nosed F11F, and did not replace the longer-nosed version until 1969. The last Tigers in service were F11As (F11F-1) of VT-26, who retired them in mid-1987.

Grumman

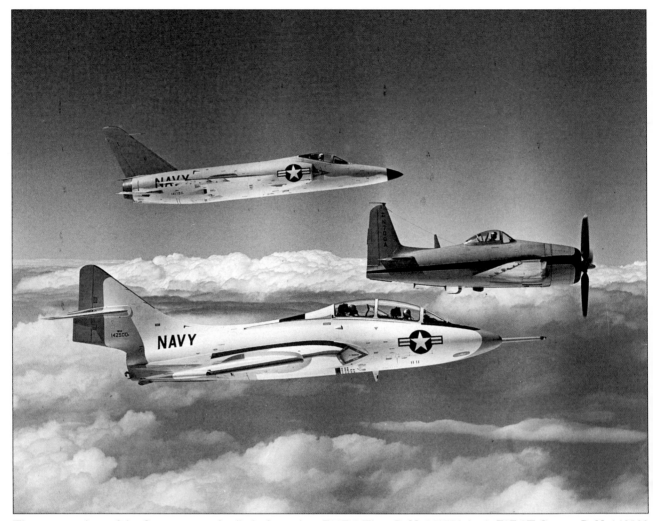

Three generations of the Grumman cat family in formation: F11F-1 Tiger BuNo141750 (top); F9F-8T Cougar BuNo142500 (in foreground); and G-58A (F8F-1B) Bearcat N700A company demonstrator, completed March 1949 (leading). (N70DA replaced G-58A (F8F-1) Gulfhawk 4 (NX120IV/NL3025), which first flew on 23 July 1947 and was destroyed in a landing accident at Elizabeth City, New Jersey.) This Bearcat, re-registered N7700C, was acquired subsequently by Cornell Laboratories, and finally passed into private ownership.

Grumman

The Beech T-34A Mentor originated from the Beech 45 Model and won the evaluation programme begun early in 1950 to select a major new primary trainer for the USN (and USAF). The T-34A led to the turboprop-powered T-34C version (pictured), service deliveries beginning in September 1976.

Beechcraft

P-3 (P3V) Orions on the flightline at Lockheed-Burbank, California. The Orion resulted from a Lockheed proposal, 1957, for maritime patrol development of the Electra airliner in response to a Navy requirement. The Lockheed proposal easily won the USN competition and the YP3V-1 (modified third Electra) flew on 19 August 1958. An initial contract for seven P3V-1s in 1960 was followed by a production run of 150 P-3As.

Lockheed via GMS

P-3A-30-L0 (P3V) Orion BuNo150525 passing a warship.

Lockheed via GMS

BuNo147864, the first of four A2F-1 development aircraft ordered in March 1959, with exhausts tilted down 23 degrees (as initially provided for Short Take-off and Landing (STOL) operation), original stabilizer location, early rudder shape, and plain fuselage brakes. This aircraft was first flown on 19 April 1960.

Grumman

A2F-1 BuNo147867, the last of the four first development batch (which was modified in December 1968 as an NA-6A to serve as a testbed for some of the Trails-Roads Interdiction Multi-Sensor (TRIM) equipment being developed for the A-6C). A second development batch of four A2F-1s was ordered in 1960 and in December 1962 BIS carrier trials were carried out on board USS *Enterprise* (CVAN-65). The A-6A Intruder (as it was redesignated in 1962) was revolutionary for several reasons, not least because it combined a Digital Integrated Attack and Navigation system (DIANE) with ground-mapping radar that made all-weather bombing possible.

Grumman

The first Intruders were taken on charge by
VA-42, the medium attack training squadron at
NAS Oceana, Virginia, in February 1963.
VA-75 'Sunday Punchers', the first operational
squadron, began receiving A-6A Intruders in
October 1963 (six A-6As of VA-75 from USS
Independence (CAV-62) are pictured).

Grumman

The North American A-5A (A3J-1) Vigilante supersonic bomber's first full squadron deployment was with VAH-7 on board the nuclear carrier *Enterprise*'s first cruise in August 1962. *Enterprise* (CVAN-65) was the world's second nuclear-powered surface warship and was commissioned in November 1961. A Vigilante could carry a 3.020 lb Mk 27 nuclear store, which was ejected rearwards from an internal linear bay, and an ASB-12 Bombing-Navigation

system allowed all-weather attacks on enemy seaports. All heavy-attack squadrons were redesignated RVAH for reconnaissance missions in 1964, all A-5As and Bs being converted to RA-5C configurations. Eighteen RA-5Cs were confirmed lost in combat in Vietnam.

North American

Although replaced aboard the larger and more modern carriers by E-2A AEW aircraft, the Grumman WF (E-18) Tracer provided AEW over the Gulf of Tonkin throughout the Vietnam War. A development of the successful C-1A Trader COD (BuNo136792 was the 41st Trader, modified as an aerodynamic prototype for the Tracer) and TF/S-2F Tracker ASW designs, E-1Bs were nicknamed 'Willy Fudds' or the 'Stoof With A Roof' (the S-2F was known as the 'Stoof', while the US2B COD version was the 'Used to Be'). The S-2 provided invaluable anti-submarine cover for CTF-77 when intervention by Chinese submarines became a possibility.

USN

A-6A BuNo152913 of VA-35 'Black Panthers' on board USS *Enterprise* (CVAN-65). Night attack specialists, VA-35 is the oldest attack squadron in the USN (formed as VB-3 in the 1930s).

Grumman

Capable of Mach 2.2, the McDonnell F-4 Phantom II resulted from a requirement for a two-seat, twin-engine, shipboard fighter, originally ordered in 1954 as a single-seat AH-1 attack aircraft. Probably the most famous of all the aircraft to emerge from the post-Korea era, the world's first truly multi-role supersonic combat aircraft flew on 27 May 1958. Pictured are two F-4Bs from VF-101 'Grim Reapers' in flight from near the Key West NAS, Florida, on 22 December 1964. Fleet deliveries of the 'Great Smoking Thunderhog' began on 8 July 1961, when VF-74's 'Bedevillers' at NAS Oceana, Virginia, began receiving F-4Bs.

USN via GMS

When war broke out in South-east Asia in 1964, F-8Es were the first aircraft to fire their guns in anger when, on 2 August, four Crusaders from *Ticonderoga*, which at the time were conducting practice firing runs near the carrier and were led by Commander James B. Stockdale, attacked North Vietnamese PT boats with 20 mm cannon and 5 inch (127 mm) Zuni rockets. On 12 June 1966 Commander Hal Marr, CO of VF-211 now aboard *Hancock*, became the first Crusader pilot to shoot down a MiG when he destroyed a MiG-17 with his second Sidewinder missile at an altitude of only 50 ft. Marr was also credited with a probable hit after blasting more MiGs with his 20 mm cannon. Nine days later, on 21 June, Marr's wingman, Lieutenant (jg) Philip V. Vampatella, shot down another MiG-17 while covering a rescue attempt to bring home an RF8 pilot shot down earlier. Crusaders were in action throughout the Vietnam War, claiming nineteen victories over MiGs between 12 June 1966 and 19 September 1968. Vought remanufactured 448 Crusaders to update their equipment and extend their service life.

via Philip Jarrett

During the 1960s, when the USN usually operated fifteen attack carriers, normally two squadrons in each Carrier Air Wing (CVW) were equipped with Douglas A-4 Skyhawks (which served alongside one squadron of A-1H Skyraiders). A-4s were among the first aircraft from TF-77 sent into action in South-east Asia. At the time of the Gulf of Tonkin incident, 2 August 1964, the only carrier within close proximity was USS *Ticonderoga* with CVW-5 which included VA-55 'Warhorses' (three A-4A Skyhawks of VA-55 are pictured here in formation) and VA-56 'Champions'. On 4 August, sixty-four aircraft, including fifteen A-4Cs from CVW-14 on board *Constellation* (CVA-64) and sixteen A-4Es of VA-55 and VA-56 from *Ticonderoga*, flew the first retaliatory strikes against North Vietnam, attacking Communist naval vessels about 70 miles off the enemy coast.

Douglas via GMS

Douglas A-1H/Js (AD-6) Skyraiders of VA-52 and VA-145 (AD-6 BuNo137567 of VA-145 is pictured) were among the first carrier-borne aircraft into action in South-east Asia when they flew the first retaliatory strikes against North Vietnam on 4 and 5 August 1964. A veteran of Korea fourteen years earlier, the 'Spad', as it was now known, still had much to offer in this present war. (A dozen squadrons were still in service aboard the fast attack carriers, the same number as at the start of the Korean War.) Skyraiders flew all manner of attack missions, starting with a strike against the Vinh oil complex on 5 August when Lieutenant (jg) Richard C. Sather, from CVW-14 on board *Constellation*, became the first Naval aviator to be killed in Vietnam. The 'Spad' was the last aircraft that did not need the aid of a steam catapult to become airborne from a carrier. With centreline fuel tanks, the Skyraider could remain airborne for 12 hours and still carry a weapon load of 8,000 lb. VA-25 'Fist of the Fleet' on board *Coral Sea* was the last Navy squadron equipped with 'Spads' and flew its final combat sortie on 20 February 1968, before retiring its Skyraiders on 10 April.

via Philip Jarrett

Four F-4s of VF-142 'Ghostriders' from *Constellation*. Phantoms first saw action in South-east Asia when F-4Bs of CVW-14 on board *Constellation* escorted the first Navy strike on 4 August 1964. The Phantom's arrival in theatre was very opportune, because, although at that time the NVAF had no fighters (they first appeared on 3 April 1965), by the end of the year thirty-four MiG-17s were available, and by June 1965 this number had increased to seventy.

USN via GMS

An A-4 Skyhawk of VF-111 'Sundowners' makes an arrested landing on board the flight deck of the attack carrier USS *Coral Sea* (CVA-43), March 1965. Affectionately known to its pilots as 'Scooter' because of the way it scooted like a balsa plane off the steam catapult, 'Heinemann's Hot Rod' (after the Douglas chief designer) became one of the most successful attack aircraft in fleet service during the period December 1962 to 1976.

USN

F-4B BuNo151485 of VF-21 'Freelancers' from USS *Midway* dive-bombing with 500 lb Snakeye retarded bombs. VF-21 F-4Bs scored the first confirmed MiG-17 victories of the war on 17 June 1965, when they attacked four NVNAF-17s south of Hanoi and brought down two with radar-guided AIM-7 Sparrow missiles. Commander Louis C. Page and his Radar Intercept Officer, Lieutenant John C. Smith Jr., together with Lieutenant Jack 'Dave' Batson and his backseater, Lieutenant Commander Robert B. Doremus, scored the victories and they were each awarded the Silver Star. On 20 June a third MiG-17 was shot down by Lieutenant Clinton B. Johnson of VA-25 'Fist of the Fleet' from *Midway*, flying a propeller-driven A-1 Skyraider. An AD-4NA flown by Lieutenant (jg) William T. Patton of VA-176 'Thunderbolts' on board *Intrepid* destroyed a MiG-17 on 9 October 1966. VA-176, flying A-6E Intruder and KA-6D tankers, was disestablished on 1 October 1991. By the end of 1965 the NVAF also had supersonic MiG-21s in its inventory.

USN via GMS

Opposite, above: Embarked on board *Independence* (CVA-62), VA-75 'Sunday Punchers', the first operational A-6 Intruder squadron, arrived in the Gulf of Tonkin in June 1965 and flew its first combat sorties on 1 July with strikes on North Vietnamese targets. In North Vietnam A-6 Intruders dropped more ordnance than USAF B-52s.

Grumman via GMS

Below: F-4Bs of VF-92 'Silver Kings' on board USS *Enterprise* (CVAN-65). Carrier fighters were first engaged in air-to-air combat on 9 April 1965, when F-4Bs of VF-96 'Fighting Falcons' from *Ranger* (CV-61) dog-fought with MiG-17s near Hainan. One enemy jet was claimed as 'probably' destroyed but one Phantom failed to return. The 'Fighting Falcons', which, along with VF-92 'Silver Kings', was disestablished in 1975, held the record for the most MiG kills of the Vietnam War. VF-96's 'Great Smoking Thunderhog' Phantoms left the fleet in 1986 and the Reserves in 1987.

USN

F-4B BuNo152227 of VF-114 'Aardvarks' landing aboard USS *Kitty Hawk* during operations in the South China Sea.

via GMS

Vietnam was the target in September 1965 for these F-4Bs, of VF-41 'Black Aces' and VF-84 'Jolly Rogers', and A-4E Skyhawks, of VA-86 'Sidewinders' and VA-72 'Blue Hawks', on board *Independence* (CAV-62).

McDonnell Douglas

Off Vietnam in September 1965 pressure builds and steam arises on the waist cat on board USS *Independence* as F-4B '211' (BuNo151478) of VF-84 'Jolly Rogers', armed with two AIM-7 Sparrow missiles, is readied for launching on signal from the Catapult Officer, kneeling at right. The steam catapult develops such brutal thrust that a loaded Phantom could be flung off at full flying speed in just 2½ seconds in a run of 200 ft.

McDonnell Douglas

F-4B BuNo151478 '211' of VF-84 'Jolly Rogers' gets airborne from the waist cat on board USS *Independence*.

McDonnell Douglas

F-4B BuNo150491 of VF-41 'Black Aces' gets airborne from USS *Independence*.

McDonnell Douglas

With everything down, F-4B BuNo151492 of VF-84 'Jolly Rogers' comes in at a steady 150 mph and prepares to slam onto the deck of *Independence* and catch the arresting wire after a sortie over Vietnam in September 1965. Once the LSO has given the order 'Clear Deck', the Phantom will be taxied away to rearm and refuel, or struck down below for heavy maintenance in the vast 3½ acre underground hangar deck.

McDonnell Douglas

An A-4E of VA-23 fires off a salvo of 3 inch rockets against Viet Cong positions, 28 October 1965.

The Vought (later LTV) A-7 Corsair II was designed to a USN requirement issued in May 1963 to replace the A-4, and the first A-7A flew on 27 September 1965. A total of 199 A-7s were built, the first being issued to VA-174, a training squadron, in October 1966. Pictured is A-7ABuNo152650 from USS *Lexington* during sea trials on the flight deck of *Independence*. VA-147 was established on 1 February 1967 and was the first fleet squadron to operate the A-7A Corsair II or 'SLUF', as it was known ('Short Little Ugly F***er'!). VA-147's SLUFs were the first deployed to Vietnam, on the carrier *Ranger* in November 1967, and they went into action over North Vietnam on 4 December.

LTV via Philip Jarrett

The turboprop-powered Grumman E-2 (W2F-1) Hawkeye, or 'Hummer', as the flying radar station is known, with its huge 24 ft diameter rotodome housing the General Electric APS96 search radar, rotating at 6 rpm, first flew on 21 October 1960. The Hawkeye has remained the airborne 'eyes of the fleet' since becoming operational with VAW-11 on board *Kitty Hawk* in the Gulf of Tonkin late in 1965. (E-2A of VAW-11 Detachment C, about to land on the USS *Kitty Hawk*, 1966, is pictured.) The designers of the E-2 did not want the vertical fins to obstruct the radar signals, though they wanted a lot of fin area in case the plane had to land with one engine shut down, so four fins were used, three of them carrying tandem-hinged rudders. To reduce radar interference, specially developed Hamilton-Standard four-bladed props have fibreglass skins over a foam core on a solid aluminium spar. The aircraft carries more than 6 tons of electronic equipment, and three radar operators facing sideways. Some fifty-nine W2F-1s/E-2As were built and forty-nine were modified to E-2B standard with a new internal software kit. In South-east Asia the Hawkeye maintained a radar watch for attacking MiGs and plotted their course, altitude, range and speed, and also directed air strikes to targets whose co-ordinates were known.

Grumman

Off Vietnam, April 1966, two F-4B Phantoms of VF-114 'Aardvarks' prepare to be catapulted from the deck of *Kitty Hawk*.

McDonnell Douglas

F-4B BuNo148373 of VF-102 'Diamondbacks' on board USS *Enterprise* is prepared for launching as a plane-guard helicopter hovers high overhead.

USN

During the Vietnam War the Sikorsky HH-3A Search and Rescue (SAR) helicopter was the primary plane-guard and combat rescue and recovery aircraft. These rescue helicopters not only operated in the Gulf of Tonkin, but also flew sorties into North Vietnam, escorted by carrier-borne fighter aircraft. Some 200 downed aircrewmen were rescued from the Gulf of Tonkin, and twenty-seven more from inland North Vietnam (where the USN lost two SAR aircraft for every three aircrewmen rescued) during ten years of war in South-east Asia. In 1972 HC-7 'Big Muthas' Det 110 alone carried out eight rescues, while HC-1 rescued thirty-six airmen and sailors.

USN

The prototype S-61 flew on 11 March 1959 and production examples (HSS-2/SH-3A Sea King) began to enter service during September 1961 with VHS-10 and VHS-3. Other models included the SH-3G utility helicopter, which evolved by stripping SH-3As of ASW equipment, and the SH-3H multi-purpose helicopter, with improved sonar, active/passive sonobouys and MAD. For the ship protection role SH-3s were equipped with Electronic Support Measures (ESM). These two SH-3As are from HS-4 'Black Knights' (established on 30 June 1952), on board USS *Yorktown*, 26 August 1966. Since late 1991 the 'Black Knights' have been flying the Sikorskyy SH-60F Seahawk ASW helicopter.

USN via GMS

An F-8E Crusader of VF-162 returns to USS *Oriskany* (CVA-34; the last of the *Essex*-class carriers) following a strike against the Viet Cong in September 1966. On 9 October Commander Richard Bellinger, CO of VF-162 and a Veteran of the Second World War and Korea, gained the Navy's first MiG-21 kill. He assumed command of CVW-16 after the CO and forty-three others (twenty-four of them aviators) were killed aboard *Oriskany* on 26 October when a fire erupted and rapidly spread below decks after a sailor accidentally ignited a magnesium flare, panicked, and then threw it into a storage locker that contain between 600 and 700 more flares. Crewmen bravely moved aircraft and over 300 bombs out of the inferno and threw them overboard. The carrier was out of action for eight months. Crusaders remained in front-line service with the USN until 2 March 1976, when *Oriskany*'s F-8Js returned from the carrier's final deployment.

USN

A P2V-7S/SP-2H Neptune, the first of which flew on 26 April 1954. The Navy received 212 P-2Hs, the last being delivered on 11 September 1962. During the Vietnam War modified P2V-7s with *Julie/Jezebel* submarine detection gear patrolled the seas of South-east Asia on 'Market Time' maritime surveillance missions. The dorsal turret was often deleted. SP-2Hs were finally retired from VP-23 in February 1970 although examples remained in Reserve squadron service until July 1980.

Lockheed

AD-6 BuNo135286 gets airborne from *Coral Sea* at 'Yankee Station' on 6 October 1966. By 1968 A-6A medium-attack squadrons had replaced all A-1 Skyraiders on carriers.

via Philip Jarrett

This badly damaged VA-212 'Rampant Raiders' A-4E Skyhawk, piloted by Lieutenant (jg) Alan R. Crebo, tried to land on the deck of USS *Bon Homme Richard* (CVA-31) after AAA fire during an attack over North Vietnam knocked off the rudder and started a fire at the wing root on 25 April 1967. His wingman, Lieutenant Graham, took this photo when Crebo tried to lower his landing gear. As only the nose wheel and tailhook would come down, a deck landing was out of the question so Crebo had to eject near the carrier, and he was picked up by helicopter. During a strike on Kep airfield on 1 May 1967 Lieutenant Commander T.R. 'Ted' Swartz in BuNo148609, a VA-76 A-4C on board USS *Bon Homme Richard*, was firing Zuni rockets at aircraft on the ground when his wingman told him there was a MiG-17 on his tail. Swartz pulled above and behind his pursuer and fired off more Zunis, which brought down the enemy jet. It was the only MiG kill by unguided rockets in the whole of the Vietnam War.

USN

Flight deck crewmen of Early Warning Squadron 33 (VAW-33) make last-minute checks on an EA-1F ECM Skyraider during flight operations aboard the ASW aircraft carrier USS *Intrepid* (CVS-11) at 'Yankee Station' on 18 September 1967, the last combat mission for a Skyraider in Vietnam. Carriers operating in support of the ground battle steamed on 'Dixie Station' in the South China Sea, and those taking part in the war against the North operated from 'Yankee Station' in the Gulf of Tonkin.

USN

A-3D2 BuNo142403 Skywarrior attack aircraft from CVW-9 comes in for recovery aboard the attack carrier USS *America* (CVA-66). Although A-3D Skywarriors of VAH squadrons flew some bombing strikes during 1965–66, it was their role as a Navy tanking aircraft from 1967 onwards which realized the 'Whale's' true potential in the Vietnam War. Ninety A-3Bs were modified as KA-3B aerial tankers or EKA-3B tanker/ECM support aircraft from 1967 to 1969. Some 'Whales' were still in service with VQ-1 and VQ-2 in 1979.

USN

Over the Mediterranean on 26 October 1967, A-4D2 (A-4B) Skyhawk BuNo142700 of VA-216 refuels an EA-3B (A3D-20) Skywarrior of VQ-2 from its 300 US gallon buddy refuelling tank. Both squadrons were part of CVW-3 stationed aboard the attack aircraft carrier USS *Saratoga* (CVA-60) during her 1967 Mediterranean deployment. Some twenty-five A3D-20/RA-3B

versions were built and they could be easily distinguished externally by the ventral 'canoe' fairing and square windows on the fuselage sides.

USN

F-4B BuNo153011 of VF-213 'Black Lions' from *Kitty Hawk* (CVA-63) dropping Mk.82 Slick 500 lb General Purpose bombs on a target in North Vietnam on 23 January 1968. Phantoms flew on bombing strikes in South-east Asia with a lead ship which signalled when to release the bomb load because the F-4 was not equipped for accurate level bomb delivery. Altogether, seventeen attack carriers (ten from the Pacific Fleet and seven from the Atlantic Fleet) were used in operations during the Vietnam War. *Hancock* established the record for the number of cruises but *Coral Sea* spent the most days on the line, with 873 days in seven cruises.

USN

Opposite, above: BuNo142650 of VAQ-135 Det 1, one of thirty-nine EKA-3B combination ECM/tanker aircraft (thirty-four of which were modified from KA3B tanker-configuration by the Naval Air Rework Facility (NARF) at Alameda, northern California). After 1975 most EKA-3Bs had their electronic equipment removed and they were redesignated KA-3Bs.

Douglas

Below: A heavily armed A-6A of VA-35 'Black Panthers' heads for a target over North Vietnam on 15 March 1968 while operating from the nuclear powered aircraft carrier USS *Enterprise* (CVAN-65) at 'Yankee Station'. Combined USN and Marine Corps A-6/KA-6D losses during the Vietnam War totalled sixty-seven aircraft.

Grumman

Two A-6A Intruders of VA-156 over the Gulf of Tonkin during a combat mission flown off USS *Constellation* (CVA-64), July 1968.
Grumman

Accelerating from 0 to 160 knots in just 4 seconds, A-6A Intruder of VA-85 'Black Falcons' takes off from the angled deck of USS *Kitty Hawk* (CVA-63) in the South China Sea.
Grumman

An A-6A Intruder of VA-85 'Black Falcons', speed-brakes extended, lands on board *Kitty Hawk*. By 1968, A-6A medium-attack squadrons had replaced all A-1 Skyraiders on carriers. Some 488 A-6A models were built before production switched to the A-6E.

Grumman

In January 1969 seven modified F-4Js were assigned 'Blue Angels', making their debut at the Marine Corps Air Station in Yuma, Arizona, on 15 March 1969, and for five seasons thrilling millions worldwide with their exhibitions of precision flying. The 'Blues' flew the Phantoms (F-4J BuNo153080 is pictured) until the end of the 1973 season when the energy crisis forced a change to the A-4F Skyhawk.

McDonnell Douglas

TA-4J Skyhawks of VT-25 'Cougars' in formation. Beginning in June 1969, 293 TA-4Js were operated by the US Naval Air Advanced Training Command. VT-25 was disestablished in 1992.

McDonnell Douglas

Grumman S2D (S2F-3S) Tracker BuNo152798 of Antisubmarine Squadron 31 (VS-31), one of sixty built for the USN, is craned on board the ASW support aircraft carrier USS *Intrepid* (CVS-11) at Quonset Point, Rhode Island, September 1969.

USN

Opposite, above: Two OV-10A Bronco VTOL aircraft of light-attack Squadron Four (VAL-4) fly low over the Mekong Delta, June 1969, in search of enemy targets.

USN

Below: 'Tell it to the Marines!' Lockheed KC-130F BuNo148895 of VMGR-152, based at MCAS Futema, Okinawa, 'tops off' an F-8J Crusader of VF-51 in the Gulf of Tonkin, August 1969. During the Vietnam War USMC KC-130 tankers were heavily committed to refuelling USN aircraft.

USN

An A-7E Corsair II of VA-27 from USS *Enterprise* in flight. The A-7B had entered combat in Vietnam on 4 March 1969 and the last of 196 -Bs was delivered in May that year. Meanwhile, the A-7D, which was built for the USAF with better electronics, Head-up Display (HUD), a more powerful TF41 engine and improved armament, was adapted for the USN and the A-7E was born.

Vought

The first fleet delivery of the A-7E was made to VA-122 in July 1969. VA-146 and VA-147's A-7Es on board USS *America* were the first to see action in Vietnam on 23 May 1970. By 1977, A-7Es equipped no less than twenty-seven light-attack squadrons, two squadrons usually operating from each carrier. Pictured is A-7E BuNo156888 with inflight refuelling probe and arrester hook lowered.

via Philip Jarrett

An A-7E of VA-147 'Argonauts' and an A-6A Intruder of VA-165 'Boomers' in flight during a combat mission in 1972. Both squadrons were part of CVW-9 assigned to *Constellation* (CVA-64). VA-165 was disestablished on 30 September 1996. VA-147 has since been redesignated VFA (strike fighter squadron), flying a new mission with CVW-9 in its F/A-18C Hornets.

USN

An A-7E Corsair II of VA-146 'Blue Diamonds' ready for launching from the flight deck of the attack carrier USS *Constellation* (CVA-64) sailing in the Gulf of Tonkin on 25 April 1972 for a strike over South Vietnam. A Corsair II could deliver 15,000 lb of bombs on target regardless of weather, thanks to its state-of-the-art continuous solution navigation and weapons systems. VA-146 has since been redesignated VFA (strike fighter squadron), flying a new mission with CVW-9 in F/A-18C Hornets.

USN

Opposite, above: An F-4H Phantom launching a Sparrow III AAM off Point Magu, California.

USN

Below: The North American (later Rockwell) T-2 Buckeye was designed to meet a USN requirement, 1956, for an all-purpose jet trainer suitable for *ab initio* training through to carrier qualification. The design used proven components like the control system similar to that used in the T-28C. The first T2J-1 (T-2A) flew for the first time on 31 January 1958. The test flight for the T-28 took place on 30 August 1962 and for the T-2C on 17 April 1968.

North American

In winter 1966 the USN issued a requirement for a VSX (Experimental carrier-based ASW aircraft) and the Lockheed YS-3A was declared the winner on 4 August 1969. The first of eight prototypes (BuNo157992) flew on 21 January 1972 and these were followed by 179 S-3A Viking production models (BuNo159410 of VS-22 'Vidars', with Texas Instruments AN/ASQ-81 MAD sensor in retractable tailboom is pictured). The Viking, or 'Hoover' as it is known (because of the sound emitted from its high-bypass-ration General Electric TF34 turbofans), first flew on 21 January 1972 and entered service in February 1974 with VS-41 'Shamrocks' training squadron at NAS North Island, San Diego, California.

Lockheed via Jerry C. Scutts

Opposite, above: R5D-3 (C-54Q) BuNo56501 was one of eighty-six C-54Ds transferred from the USAF to the USN. Most surviving R5D-3s were redesignated C-54Qs in 1962.

McDonnell Douglas

Below: Turboprop Beech T-44A (Super King Air) 0842 in flight. Eleven UC-12Ms are still used by the USN for liaison and communications.

Beechcraft

P-3A-60-LO Orion BuNo152182 of VP-10 'Red Lancers' on patrol from Brunswick, Maine. The 'Red Lancers' were established on 19 March 1951, flying Lockheed P2V Neptunes from Jacksonville, Florida, before moving to Brunswick and receiving their first P-3A in 1965. VP-10's first P-3B arrived in 1966, and first P-3C Update in 1980.

USN via GMS

An Ordnance
loading a sonobouy
aboard a P-3.
    USN via GMS

A P-3 Orion tactical compartment.
USN via GMS

At the end of the 1973 season the 'Blue Angels' flight demonstration team changed from the F-4J to the F-4F Skyhawk, seen here in a delta formation with NPTR El Centro in the background. The team's A-4Fs had their armament removed, their J52-P-8As replaced by more powerful J52-P-408As, and smoke generating cannisters installed. The A-4Fs were used until 1987 when they were exchanged for F/A-18As.

McDonnell Douglas

The last operational TF-9J Cougars of VT-4 prepare to make their final launch from USS *John F. Kennedy* in February 1974, bringing a seventeen-year career with the Naval Air Training Command to an end.

Grumman

P-3C Orion BuNo157321 of VP-56 'Dragons'. This unit, based at NAS Jacksonville, Florida, disbanded on 28 June 1991.

USN photo by Phan Kirk M. Fasking

In USN service the C-9B transport (derivation of the DC-9 Series 20 airliner) is operated by eight USN squadrons. BuNo159116 of VR-57 is pictured over *Queen Mary*, berthed at Long Beach, California.

USN

A-6E Intruders of VA-42 'Green Pawns' in formation. First rolled off the production line in Bethpage, New York, in 1970, the A-6E differed from the A-6A as it has an AN/ASQ-133 solid-state digital computer and AN/APQ-148 multi-mode radar in place of the computer and search and track radar. Total output of the A-6E reached 195 built on the production lines, while 240 A-6As, A-6Bs and A-6Cs were subsequently brought up to A-6E standard. In the late 1980s, Intruders were given a new composite wing by the Boeing Corporation to extend their service life to 8,800 flight hours.

Grumman

Opposite: F-4Js of VX-4 'The Evaluators' Air Test and Evaluation Squadron in formation, BuNo153783 with *Playboy* insignia on the tail and the furthest bedecked in a 1976 bicentennial colour scheme. BuNo153783 first flew from St Louis on 18 March 1967 and was issued to VX-4 at Point Magu, California, where the Phantom became one of the most celebrated of the F-4s, known as the 'Black Bunny' because of its all-black scheme. The 'Black Bunny' remained with VX-4 all its Navy life and retained this famous scheme for most of that time, only resorting to low visibility grey in October 1980. It was retired and sent to Davis Monthan in February 1982. After being taken out of storage in 1984, the 'Black Bunny' became ZE352 in RAF service after refurbishment – one of fifteen F-4Js acquired for the RAF in 1984 to equip a new squadron (No. 74) to replace the Phantoms of No. 29 Squadron, which was detached to the South Atlantic following the Falklands War.

McDonnell Douglas

The first of two Grumman YE-2C prototypes, converted from E-2A Hawkeye airframes, flew on 20 January 1971. E-2C production versions differ from the E-2A/B with more powerful engines as well as improved detection capability, reliability and maintainability. E-2Cs were first delivered to VAW-123 at NAS Norfolk in November 1973 and this squadron first deployed with its new Hawkeyes on board *Saratoga* in September 1974. E-2C BuNo159501 of VAW-126 from USS *Constellation* is pictured.

Grumman

Opposite: Four early Grumman F-14As in formation. The Tomcat – the last naval aircraft in the famous Grumman cat family – was a result of an early 1960s USN requirement for a high-performance fighter to replace the aging F-4 Phantom. The first of twelve research and development aircraft made its maiden flight on 21 December 1970 and the first production aircraft was delivered to the USN in June 1972. For two years an evaluation of the type was carried out.

Grumman

BuNo158614, one of three early F-14As delivered in late 1972, is safely 'trapped' on board USS *Forrestal* during initial carrier trials at sea in June 1972 and comes to a halt at the end of its landing run.

Grumman

Opposite, above: F-14A BuNo160919 from VF-32 'Swordsmen', carrying six AIM-54C Phoenix long-range AAMs beneath its wings and fuselage centreline.

Grumman

Below: An F-14A launches a AIM-54 Phoenix missile. While the Tomcat can carry up to six of these $1 million missiles, because of weight considerations during recovery back aboard a carrier the F-14 usually carries just two, on the forward stations LAU-93s. Main missile armament comprises four AIM-7E Sparrow MRAAMs partially recessed under the fuselage or four Phoenix mounted below. In addition, four AIM-9L/M Sidewinder SRAAMs, or two Sidewinders plus two Phoenix or two Sparrow, can be carried on two underwing pylons.

Grumman

An F-14A of the famous VF-14 'Tophatters', which began receiving its first Tomcats in January 1973, replacing the squadron's F-4B Phantoms. (VF-14 is the oldest squadron in the Navy, with a continuous history stretching back to 1919.)

Grumman

When the Tomcat began an eight-month deployment to the Western Pacific with VF-1 'Wolfpack' and VF-2 'Bounty Hunters' on board the 90,000 ton, nuclear-powered *Enterprise* (CVAN-65) in mid-September 1974, it was the world's first operational air superiority fighter with a variable-sweep wing. (VF-1 and VF-2 were established at Miramar, California, on 14 October 1972, and received their first Tomcats on 1 July 1973.) VF-1 and VF-2 moved to USS *Ranger* (CV-61) in September 1980, joining CVW-2, cruising on board *Kitty Hawk* in early 1984 before returning to *Ranger*. F-14A '213' from VF-2 is pictured landing on *Ranger*, the arrester hook about to catch the No. 4 wire. CV-61 was decommissioned in 1993.

Grumman

DC-130A BuNo158228 of Fleet Composite Squadron -3 (VC-3), armed with three BQM-34 Firebee target drones, August 1975. This aircraft was retired in 1979. Avtel Services Inc., of Mojave, California, continues to operate DC-130As on Teledyne Ryan and Northrop drone operations for the USN.

USN

Lockheed EC-130Q BuNo159469 was one of eighteen improved TACAMO (Take Charge And Move Out) airborne communications aircraft and was delivered to VQ-4 at NAS Patuxent River, Maryland, in July 1975. (Four EC-130Gs had been modified during 1966 to 1970.) EC-130Qs operated by both VQ-3 at NAS Agana, Guam (later, NAS Barbers Point, Hawaii), and VQ-4 acted as relay stations by receiving VLF and UHF communications from the National Command Authority (NCA) Airborne National Command Posts (ABNCPs) via satellites and other emergency radio links, and then retransmitting the instructions in VLF to ballistic missile submarines at sea. Boeing E-6As gradually replaced the EC-130Qs during 1989 to 1992.

Lockheed

VF-14's 'Tophatters' and VF-32's 'Swordsmen', which exchanged its F-4B Phantoms for Tomcats in 1974, were the first Atlantic Fleet units equipped with the Tomcat, and they went to sea aboard *John F. Kennedy* in June 1975, to take up station with the Sixth Fleet in the Mediterranean. Pictured landing aboard the 'Big John' is an F-14A of VF-32.

Grumman

An F-14A Tomcat from VF-51 'Screaming Eagles', which began replacing its F-4N Phantoms on 16 June 1978. The 'Eagles' first cruise was with CVW-15 on board USS *Kitty Hawk* (CV-63) in May 1979.

Grumman

Between the early 1980s and the early 1990s, the Sixth Fleet was on station during an uneasy peace between Libya and the US. Pictured are four F-14As of VF-32 'Swordsmen' overflying *John F. Kennedy*. (The 'Swordsmen' were embarked for three Mediterranean cruises with CVW-1 on board the 'Big John', beginning in 1981, before moving to CVW-6 on board *Independence*.) Long-range bombers armed with sea-skimming missiles pose the main threat to Navy vessels and only the F-14 Tomcat can intercept them before they get in range. On 19 August 1981 F-14As from VF-41 'Black Aces', operating from the *Nimitz*, shot down two Libyan Sukhoi Su-22s that were approaching the battle-group in a hostile manner.

Grumman

A-6E BuNo155673 TRAM (Target Recognition and Attack Multi-sensor, which provides television-type imagery of targets not detectable visually or by radar, coupled with laser-guided weapon delivery). Note the TRAM turret under the nose which houses Forward Looking Airborne Radar (FLIR) equipment first tested on an A-6E in October 1974. In March 1986, during the PRAIRIE FIRE Operation launched to provoke Libya into a direct military confrontation, two A-6E Intruders sank a Libyan fast attack craft with AGM84A Harpoon anti-ship missiles and Rockeye cluster bombs.

Grumman

BENINA AIRFIELD
15 APR 86

DESTROYED F-27

DAMAGED MI-8/HIP

DESTROYED MI-8/HIP

On 14 April 1986 Operation EL DORADO CANYON, the American bombing of terrorist-related targets in Libya, went ahead. Targets for the fourteen A-6Es from USS *America* and USS *Coral Sea* in the eastern Mediterranean were the Al Jumahiriya barracks in Benghazi and Benina airport outside the city. The Intruders destroyed at least four MiG-23s, a Fokker F-27 and two Mil Mi-8 helicopters at Benina airfield (pictured). Overall, EL DORADO CANYON was a great success. Two days after the attacks, post-strike reconnaissance by two SR-71As confirmed that all five targets had been well hit.

USN

F-14As of VF-74 'Bedevillers' in formation. VF-74 began replacing its F-4S Phantoms in June 1983 and the squadron became fully operational on the Tomcat in October, going to sea on board *Saratoga* in April 1984. The 'Bedevillers' flew against Libya in Operation PRAIRIE FIRE in March 1986 and Operation EL DORADO CANYON on 14 April 1986.

Grumman

Part of the air component for EL DORADO CANYON were six F/A18A Hornets from *Coral Sea*, which, together with six A-7Es from USS *America*, blasted the SAM and radar installations with Shrike and HARM air-to-surface missiles at Libyan air defence sites along the coast and in and around Benghazi. The Hornet was conceived as a multi-mission aircraft to supercede the F-4 Phantom fighter, A-4 Skyhawk and A-7E attack aircraft, in USMC and USN squadrons (redesignated VFA (Strike-Fighter)). The prototype (BuNo160775) was rolled out at St Louis on 13 September 1978 and first flew on 18 November.

Pictured in June 1981 is F/A-18 Hornet BuNo161250 of Fleet Replacement Training Squadron VFA-125 at NAS Lemoore, California, with A-7E BuNo158009 from the same unit. Hornets first went to sea in February 1985 with VFA-25 'Fist of the Fleet' and VFA-113 'Stingers', part of CVW-14 aboard *Constellation* (CV-64).

McDonnell Douglas via Philip Jarrett

Following Operation EL DORADO CANYON, F/A-18C Hornets of VFA-86 'Sidewinders' (pictured) replaced A-7Es aboard USS *America* and these were on board the carrier with the rest of CVW-1 during deployment in the Gulf Crisis, November 1990.

McDonnell Douglas

Derived from the successful Grumman A-6 design, the EA-6B Prowler's forward fuselage is stretched to accommodate a second cockpit for two EW operators and the rear fuselage is extended to balance the aircraft. Prowler is the standard USN carrier-borne ECM aircraft and is intended to confuse, and identify, enemy radars, and assist and escort friendly combat aircraft. The EA-6B first flew on 25 May 1968, and delivery of the first production models began in 1971 (BuNo158033 of VAQ-132 is pictured). The new Prowler represented a dramatic improvement over the original EA-6A, which had first flown in 1963. EA-6B Prowlers took part in EL DORADO CANYON, being used to carry out ECM jamming of Libyan radars while the strike force attacked. In the Gulf War, 16 January to 28 February 1991, an EA-6B EW squadron was included in each Carrier Air Wing on board the Navy carriers.

Grumman

In 1986 the Navy flight demonstration squadron the 'Blue Angels' replaced its A-4Fs and began training with F/A-18As that winter for the 1987 season (pictured).

USN

Opposite, above: The Rolls-Royce Dart propeller-turbine powered G-159 Gulfsteam I first flew (N701G) on 14 August 1958, and 200 were built over eleven years, 190 of them as executive transports. Of the ten military models produced, one VC-4A served the US Coast Guard, and nine TC-4C 'flying classrooms' served in the USN to train bombardier/navigators flying A-6 Intruders. Pictured is TC-4C BuNo155725 of VA-128 with TRAM turret, at NAS Whidbey Island, Washington, in August 1989.

Author

Below: Lieutenant (jg) Pamela Redford conducts a pre-flight check in the cockpit of her C-2A Greyhound at NAS North Island, California, 10 April 1992. Lieutenant Commander Barbara Rainey, née Allen, was the USN's first woman naval aviator when she received her wings of gold and commission at Corpus Christi on 22 February 1974. Later assigned duty in the Training Command as an instructor, Rainey was killed in a training accident on 13 July 1982 at Whiting Field, becoming the USN's first female naval aviator to die in an aircraft accident. VRC-40's Lieutenant Donna Spruill was the first female to qualify for carrier landings in a fixed wing aircraft when she completed Car-Quals in a Grumman C-1A on board *Independence* on 20 June 1979. Ensign Brenda E. Robinson was the first black woman to become a naval aviator on 6 June 1980. She also joined VRC-40 at Norfolk to fly the C-1A.

USN

USS *America* (CV-66; pictured at St Thomas, US Virgin Islands, 3 May 1993) was commissioned into the Atlantic Fleet in January 1965, operating on the east coast and in the Mediterranean. In 1975 she was modified to operate F-14s and ASW S-3A aircraft. CV-66 served in the Gulf War, arriving in theatre in January 1991 and launching aircraft from CVW-1 as part of Operation DESERT STORM. She was decommissioned in 1996.

via Walt Truax

F-14D (A+) is a much improved Tomcat version with advanced avionics and weapons systems and more powerful engines. Although it arrived too late to see action in the Gulf War, no fewer than eight F014A and two F-14B Tomcat squadrons were deployed aboard five carriers during the conflict. During a reconnaissance mission over Western Iraq on 21 January 1991, *Saratoga*'s CVW-17 lost an F-14B from VF-103 'Sluggers' and an F/A-18C, both to SAMs. This was the only occasion a Tomcat was lost during DESERT STORM. The pilot, Lieutenant Devon Jones, was picked up by helicopter and Lieutenant Laurence Slade, his back-seater, was taken prisoner. On 6 February Lieutenant Stuart Broce and Commander Ron McElraft of VF-1 'Wolfpack' from CVW-2 on board USS *Ranger* destroyed a Mi-8 helicopter with a single AIM-9 Sidewinder. It was one of only three victories claimed by USN aviation in the Gulf War.

Grumman

A heavily armed trio of F-14A Tomcats from VF-84 'Jolly Rogers' bank above cloud layer. 'Fighting 84' is the latest squadron to inherit VF-17's famous 'Jolly Rogers' skull and crossbones (see opposite, below). Home-ported to NAS Oceana, Virginia, the Tactical Air Reconnaissance Pod System-equipped (TARPS) squadron is assigned to CVW-8 on board USS *Theodore Roosevelt*. Late in 1994, VF-84 Tomcats supported USAF Fighter Weapons School opertions at Nellis AFB, Nevada, and participated in avionics test and tactics development exercise with the 422nd T&E Squadron, flying both as adversaries and 'Blue Air'. The 'Jolly Rogers' flew more than 100 missions with a 90 per cent sortie completion rate.

via Lee Cook

F/A-18C Hornet from VFA-131 'Wildcats' takes on fuel from an S-3B Viking from VS-31 'Topcats' while flying over the Arabian Gulf, 26 March 1996. Both units are part of CVW-7 on board *George Washington*.

USN

USS *John F. Kennedy* (CV-67) on 10 December 1996 showing the 4.56 acres and 1,0511/2 ft × 252 ft deck area to good advantage as it steams in the Northern Puerto Rican Operations Area (NPOA) during carrier air wing qualifications. President Kennedy's daughter Caroline, the ship's sponsor, christened and launched the carrier on 27 May 1967. Entering naval service on 7 September 1968, 'Big John' has spent much of her career in the Mediterranean, completing fourteen deployments by 1993. On 16 January 1991 aircraft from the ship's CVW-3 began Operation DESERT STORM with attacks on Iraqi forces. *Kennedy* launched 114 strikes and 2,895 sorties with the aircrews of CVW-3, mainly from the Red Sea, flying 11,263 combat hours and delivering more than 3.5 million lb of ordnance in the conflict, during which CVW-3 made the first operational use of the SLAM missile.

USN–Photographer's Mate 2nd Class Scott A. Moak

Cooks aboard USS *John F. Kennedy* preparing early breakfast. With the air wing embarked, a carrier has 5,222 hungry mouths to feed and the mess crews have to prepare 15,666 meals daily.

Author

USN test pilot Lieutenant Tom Hole fires an AIM-9 Sidewinder missile from the Super Hornet F/A-18F(2) during tests conducted out of NAS Patuxent River, Maryland. The F/A-18C flew for the first time on 3 September 1987. This version has the capability to carry the Advanced Medium-Range Air-to-Air Missile (AMRAAM), the Maverick air-to-ground missile, and the infra-red imaging self-protection jammer. The first F/A-18C was delivered to the USN on 23 September 1987. MDC rolled out the first improved F-18E/F on 18 September 1995, with a first flight in November. The USN plans to acquire 1,000 F-18E/Fs to replace early F/A-18A/Bs and F-14s. Initial operational capability is planned for 2004. The Super Hornet is the USN's newest Strike Fighter and replaced the A-6 Intruder; it is also the future programmed replacement for the Tomcat.

USN

A RIM-7 'Sea Sparrow' missile is launched from its Mk.29 launcher on board USS *John C. Stennis* (CVN-74) during a missile exercise, 27 August 1997. Two Mk.29 launchers are located on the stern at either edge of the flight deck, the third is situated on a sponson on the starboard forward deck. 'Sea Sparrow' is also used for the Basic Point Missile Defence System (BPDMS) for anti-ship missile defence.

USN–Photographer's Mate 3rd Class Prather.

Commander John 'Saddam' Husaim and Lieutenant Wayne 'Gooch' Gutierrez, from HS-3 'Tridents' on board *John F. Kennedy* on patrol in the Sikorsky SH-60F Ocean Hawk. Each helicopter squadron on board the carrier flies SH-60F and HH-60H Seahawks. The SH-60F is the Navy's CV Inner Zone antisubmarine helicopter to protect the Carrier Battle Group (CBG) from close-in enemy submarines. The HH-60H is a combat SAR and special support helicopter.

Author

EA-6B Prowler 620 of VAQ-141 'Shadowhawks' on the deck of USS *John F. Kennedy*. The crew comprises a pilot and three ECM officers. ECMO 1 in the forward starboard station provides navigation duties and works the Raytheon AN/ALQ-99F deception jamming system, while ECMOs 3 and 4 in the rear compartment work the AN/ALQ99 TJS (Tactical Jamming System).

Author

Quality Check personnel go about their tasks in front of a VFA-15 'Valions' F/A-18C at the end of another long, but rewarding day on board USS *John F. Kennedy*. The average age of sailors on board is just nineteen.

Author

EA-6B BuNo161352 '621' of VAQ-141 'Shadowhawks' is trapped on board *John F. Kennedy*. The small prong at the base of the refuelling probe and the fairing at the base of the large tailfin pod (which houses the main SIR (System Integration Receivers) antennas to detect enemy radars) house the ALQ-126 DECM (Deception ECM) system that interrupts and confuses enemy radars. Externally, up to four AGM-88A HARM anti-radiation missiles can be carried below the wings, together with AN/ALQ-99 emitter pods, or Aero-1D 300 US gallon drop tanks. A further AN/ALQ-99 pod is carried on the centreline pylon. To reduce the load on the Prowler's electrical generating system, each pod has its own generator, driven by a ram air turbine on the nose of the pod. The pods were initially designed to jam a specific waveband, but the new ICAP-2 (increased capability) version has pods that can jam in any two of seven wavebands.

Author

'Fly 1' motions a VFA-15 'Valions' F/A-18C away shortly after being trapped aboard *John F. Kennedy*. Each arrester wire has a tensile strength of 176,000 lb. Regular checks are made to make sure that they are not about to snap. After 100 'traps', a wire is removed and thrown overboard to ensure that it is never mistakenly fitted and used again. The arrester hook takes a 50 ton load when the wire is engaged. As soon as the 22 ton aircraft slams onto the deck (placing an 80 ton load on the undercarriage, 30 tons on the nosewheel, and each ton of stores a 10-ton load), the Tomcat pilot (who, along with his RIO, has just absorbed a 1½ ton load) has to open the throttles to full power in case he has to 'bolter'. This occurs when the arrester wires are missed and he is forced to power out on a touch and go.

Author

A VF-41 'Black Aces' F-14A is towed away on the deck of *John F. Kennedy* as a VFA-87 'Golden Warriors' F/A-18 taxies past the line of Hornets on the aft deck.

Author

A lightly loaded F/A-18C Hornet can be launched without using afterburner. Its two General Electric F404-GE-402 afterburning low-bypass turbofans are rated at about 16,000 lb, more than adequate when hauling a normal take-off load of 36,710 lb for a typical fighter mission, or 49,224 lb for an attack mission.

Author

A VFA-15 'Valions' F/A-18C Hornet carrying centreline and underwing fuel tanks and LAU-10 rocket launchers taxies by the 300 ft long waist cats where a VF-41 'Black Aces' F-14A and an F/A-18C of VFA-87 'Golden Warriors', in front of a raised JBD, await launching. The 'Golden Warriors' and the 'Valions' are homeported at NAS Cecil Field, Jacksonville, Florida. Both squadrons took part in DESERT STORM, flying missions as part of CVW-8 on board USS *Theodore Roosevelt*.

Author

S-3B Vikings of VS-24 'Scouts' taxi back on board *Kennedy* after landing flanked by a 'Black Aces' F-14A Tomcat and Grumman C-2A Greyhound of Fleet Tactical Support Squadron Forty (VRC–40) 'Rawhides'. Arrival on board carriers at sea is usually made in the C-2A or COD. VRC-40, previously known as 'Codfish Airlines', was established on 1 July 1960 and operates the Greyhound for COD support in the Atlantic Fleet. (VR-24 (Fleet Logistic Support Squadron) 'Lifting Eagles', which calls itself 'The Biggest Little Airline', also carries out transport duties with C-2A and CT-39G Sabreliner aircraft for carriers in the Mediterranean from NAS Sigonella in Sicily.) Note the AIM-9L Sidewinder on the port side of the Tomcat and the nose-mounted M61A-1 Vulcan 20 mm cannon. The nose of the F-14A also houses the Hughes AWG-9 radar and fire-control system, which is capable of picking out and tracking low-flying aircraft against ground or sea clutter. The chin housing accommodates an ECM antenna in the lower section and the cylindrical casing above contains a Northrop AXX-1 stabilized, telephoto video camera (TV Camera Set (TCS) with a range in excess of 10 miles), which is steered by the radar.

Author

A VF-14 'Topcatters' F-14A hurtles off the bow of *John F. Kennedy* in the Mediterranean, October 1997, using the full 20,900 lb afterburning thrust that is available from the two Pratt & Whitney TF30s. (Some of the early accidents involving Tomcats with TF30 engines arose from compressor stall when applying afterburner during launch.) The F-14A goes from 0 to 150 knots in 2.2 seconds. At sea level the Tomcat can climb at up to 30,000 ft a minute. Take-offs from carriers in the later marks of Tomcat with their two General Electric F1210s, rated at 23,100 lb afterburning thrusts, can safely be made dry, without afterburner.

Author

Opposite: An ES-3A Shadow of VQ-6 (Fleet Air Reconnaissance squadron) 'Ravens' completes its landing run. In the foreground is a E-2C Hawkeye of VAW-124 (Carrier AEW Squadron 124) 'Bear Aces' carrying more than 6 tons of electronic equipment, and three radar operators facing sideways. During DESERT STORM the 'Bear Aces' operated from USS *Theodore Roosevelt*. For easy storage, the Hawkeye's wings twist and fold backwards while the rotodome can be lowered hydraulically. Like the C-2A, the E-2 is the only aircraft operating from the deck of a ship that does not have rocket-powered ejection seats. The ES-3A is the newest edition to the Navy's carrier wings, providing the battle group with electronic surveillance (ELINT), including intercept of enemy communications (COMINT).

Author

A VF-14 'Topcatters' F-14A soars away into the sky after take-off. The aircraft is held against full thrust by a retaining link behind the nosewheel attached to the catapult shuttle that snaps off as the catapult reaches its full working pressure. All four catapults under the deck comprise two 300 ft cylinders, each with a metal valve running along its entire length. To give some idea of the power of the device, if one could mount a Volkswagen Beetle and catapult it, the car would 'fly' for 12 miles! Pilots call being launched off a carrier the 'E-ticket ride' after the No. 1 ride at Disneyworld.

Author

A VF-14 'Topcatters' F-14A comes to an abrupt halt just short of the forward deck after being trapped aboard *John F. Kennedy*. Final approach for Tomcat pilots is usually flown with a sink rate of 750 ft per minute and this is calculated to bring the F-14 down to engage the third of the four arrester wires. A Tomcat's great 64 ft 1½ inch wing with flaps extending across the full span are an enormous aid to recovery and the aircraft is typically trapped at 130 knots or less on landing and the F-14 comes to a dead stop from its approach speed in only 2 seconds. Even so, the aircraft appears *every* time to finish very close to the end of the ramp!

Author

A pair of S-3B Vikings of VS-24 (Sea-Control Squadron 24) 'Scouts' about to be catapulted off the bow cats of *John F. Kennedy*. VS-24 was established on 25 May 1960 and is homeported at NAS Cecil Field, Jacksonville, Florida. During DESERT STORM the 'Scouts', part of CVW-8 on board *Theodore Roosevelt*, operated as 'ground attack Vikings' armed with Mk 82 500 lb bombs and other ordnance, flying bombing missions against Iraqi ground as well as sea targets.

Author

Sikorsky SH-60F Ocean Hawk of HS-3 'Tridents' on board *John F. Kennedy* prepares to take-off.

Author

Fish-eye lens shot of the forward deck of *John F. Kennedy*.

Author

Keeping Watch. Aboard USS *George Washington* on 17 February 1998, LSOs of CVW-1 evaluate an ES-3A Shadow landing on board. CVW-1 and *George Washington* were deployed to the Persian Gulf in support of Operation SOUTHERN WATCH.

USN–Photographer's Mate 3rd Class Brian Fleske

INDEX